Exciting new resources for readers:

The 3rd edition of *Principles of Management Essentials You Always Wanted To Know* has some exciting new additions!

- This edition has a new chapter called International Business and Management. In this chapter, you will get a peek into the possibilities of taking your business international and the various factors that will stimulate its growth or inhibit it.

- Each chapter has concise 'Key Learning Objectives' that will give you an overview of what you will learn in the chapter.

- Each chapter has 5 multiple-choice quizzes to test your knowledge and complete the circle of learning.

Vibrant Publishers is committed to publishing books that are content-rich, concise, and approachable, enabling more readers to read and make the fullest use of them. We hope this book provides you with the most enriching learning experience.

Feel free to email us at reachus@vibrantpublishers.com if you have any questions/suggestions.

SELF-LEARNING MANAGEMENT SERIES

TITLE	PAPERBACK* ISBN
AGILE ESSENTIALS	9781636510057
BUSINESS PLAN ESSENTIALS	9781636511214
BUSINESS STRATEGY ESSENTIALS	9781949395778
COST ACCOUNTING AND MANAGEMENT ESSENTIALS	9781636511030
DATA ANALYTICS ESSENTIALS	9781636511184
DECISION MAKING ESSENTIALS	9781636510026
DIGITAL MARKETING ESSENTIALS	9781949395747
DIVERSITY IN THE WORKPLACE ESSENTIALS	9781636511122
FINANCIAL ACCOUNTING ESSENTIALS	9781636510972
FINANCIAL MANAGEMENT ESSENTIALS	9781636511009
HR ANALYTICS ESSENTIALS	9781636510347
HUMAN RESOURCE MANAGEMENT ESSENTIALS	9781949395839
LEADERSHIP ESSENTIALS	9781636510316
MARKETING MANAGEMENT ESSENTIALS	9781949395792
MICROECONOMICS ESSENTIALS	9781636511153
OPERATIONS AND SUPPLY CHAIN MANAGEMENT ESSENTIALS	9781949395242
ORGANIZATIONAL BEHAVIOR ESSENTIALS	9781636510378
PRINCIPLES OF MANAGEMENT ESSENTIALS	9781636511542
PROJECT MANAGEMENT ESSENTIALS	9781636510712
SALES MANAGEMENT ESSENTIALS	9781636510743

*Also available in Hardback & Ebook formats

BUY 3 FOR THE PRICE OF 2
USE DISCOUNT CODE 3FOR2

Offer valid only on
www.vibrantpublishers.com

SELF-LEARNING MANAGEMENT SERIES

PRINCIPLES OF MANAGEMENT ESSENTIALS
YOU ALWAYS WANTED TO KNOW

A pragmatic guidebook for ushering into the role of a manager

CALLIE DAUM

Principles of Management Essentials You Always Wanted To Know

Third Edition

© 2022, By Vibrant Publishers, USA. All rights reserved. No part of this publication may be reproduced or distributed in any form or by any means, or stored in a database or retrieval system, without the prior permission of the publisher.

Paperback ISBN 10: 1-63651-154-6
Paperback ISBN 13: 978-1-63651-154-2

Ebook ISBN 10: 1-63651-155-4
Ebook ISBN 13: 978-1-63651-155-9

Hardback ISBN 10: 1-63651-156-2
Hardback ISBN 13: 978-1-63651-156-6

Library of Congress Control Number: 2018903899

This publication is designed to provide accurate and authoritative information in regard to the subject matter covered. The Author has made every effort in the preparation of this book to ensure the accuracy of the information. However, information in this book is sold without warranty either expressed or implied. The Author or the Publisher will not be liable for any damages caused or alleged to be caused either directly or indirectly by this book.

Vibrant Publishers books are available at special quantity discount for sales promotions, or for use in corporate training programs. For more information please write to bulkorders@vibrantpublishers.com

Please email feedback / corrections (technical, grammatical or spelling) to spellerrors@vibrantpublishers.com

To access the complete catalogue of Vibrant Publishers, visit www.vibrantpublishers.com

About the Author

Callie Daum has worked in the healthcare industry for over 20 years gaining experience in managing teams, project management, strategic development and implementation, business marketing to increase revenues, and many more lessons learned on how to thrive in a business industry. As a seasoned Senior Project Manager and Leader, her goals include adding value, working efficiently and effectively, and sharing best practices to achieve overall success. Callie started her career as an Application Analyst at Computer Sciences Corporation, before moving on to project management and leadership at Cerner Corporation, Atrium Health, and Novant Health. Callie is a certified Project Management Professional, Professional Scrum Master, Certified Health Coach, and received a certificate in Master Level Six Sigma at Villanova University.

Other contributors

We would like to thank Prof. Fernando Pargas for contributing the chapter 'International Business and Management.' Fernando is a Management Professor at James Madison University and has taught various subjects like International Marketing, International Management, Business Strategy, and Organizational Behavior. He was a member of the United States Chamber of Commerce International Policy Committee.

We would like to thank Dr. Mark Koscinski for contributing text on Decision Making Techniques in Chapter 3, Planning and Decision Making. Dr. Mark Koscinski CPA D.Litt. is an assistant professor of accounting practice at Moravian College in Bethlehem, Pennsylvania where he teaches a wide variety of accounting and management courses. Prior to joining Moravian College, Mark had significant experience in public and private accounting. He has been the chief financial officer of a publicly traded defense contractor and a privately held toy company.

What experts say about this book!

The book is a comprehensive coverage of what one would like to know about management and its sub disciplines. Students and managers will find the book very useful as it is an easy and simple read. The topics covered are current and provide appropriate depth with examples.

**– Subrat Sarangi, Fellow in Management
XLRI, Jamshedpur**

The author Callie Daum and other contributors have maintained a comprehensive layout and lucid language with adequate content throughout the book. The chapter summaries will suffice the students to retrieve the full contents of the entire chapter in an invigorating way. The quizzes at the end of each chapter will work as an intellectual exercise to the students and professionals alike.

This will be a valuable document for the undergraduate and postgraduate students and a guide to a spectrum of learners from those in the foundation stage to the practicing professionals.

**– K.X. Joseph, Dean, Faculty of Commerce & Professional Studies,
Rajagiri College of Social Sciences**

This book teaches practical business terms and concepts that every businessman should know in a simple and understandable language. As a teacher, I would suggest all the entry level management students to read this book, to clearly understand management terminologies with no confusion.

**– Rajkalaiselvi M, Assistant Professor,
Justice Basheer Ahmed Sayeed College for Women**

What experts say about this book!

The book is easy to comprehend. It covers topics which are useful to both management experts and new managers alike. The short and concise texts with illustrations makes this book engaging. I shall be using this book for my management courses.

– Manish Kiling, Assistant Professor
Gauhati University

Principles of Management has covered all the aspects of management and is easy to understand even by an undergraduate student. This book will be useful for undergraduate students, managers, teachers and research scholars. It can be prescribed for undergraduate courses too. The Self-Learning Management series as a whole would be a great help for the student as well as the professional community.

– Mrs. Ritika Waghray, Assistant Professor
St.Joseph's Degree & PG College

Callie Daum's Principles of Management Essentials book provides startup founders and management students a thorough understanding of managerial concepts. It is simple to understand, well-structured with flow charts and covers a wide range of business topics such as Human Resource Management, Quality Management, Customer Relationship Management and International Business and Management. This book guides the readers through the real-world application of management skills. All the books in the Self- Learning Management series of Vibrant Publishers give clear insights on all subject areas of management, and can be used by undergraduate and postgraduate students.

– K.Mathumathi, Assistant Professor,
Agurchand Manmull Jain College

What experts say about this book!

This book has a relatively complete compilation of managerial information. "Principles of Management Essentials You Always Wanted to Know" is an exceptional book that covers all of the pertinent and most important components of the management stream. In today's global context, such publications help managers be better leaders and provide vital guidance in this modern era. The wider typography, as well as the inclusion of charts, graphs, and illustrations makes the book very reader-oriented. This will undoubtedly be one of the best management books for students, researchers, entrepreneurs, marketers, and even beginners because it combines contemporary knowledge with simple language. I would strongly suggest this book to my students, colleagues, and aspiring managers.

– Hetal Rathod, Assistant Professor
Gujarat Technological University

Principles of Management Essentials by Callie Daum, a book in the Self-Learning Management series lives up to the promises made. It covered 18 broad essential topics for a manager to refer to in the discharge of their responsibilities. The focus on the basics of communication and change management reflects the need of the hour for managers. The team management and group handling skills needed is rounded off with a discussion on organization culture.
The author has done an appreciable job of bringing together the topics in a practical manner. The book is easy to read and will help not only self learning managers but also management students as a ready reckoner. The book addresses a niche need of understanding the concepts driving managers in the data driven dynamic business arena. It is a must read for any one looking to learn the latest thoughts on essential areas of management literature.

– Dr. Nagapavan Chintalapati
Central University of Jharkhand

This page is intentionally left blank

Table of Contents

1 Introduction to Management   1
    1.1 Management Types   2
    1.2 Authority   4
    Chapter Summary   6
    Quiz   8

2 Functions of Management   11
    2.1 Planning   12
    2.2 Organizing   13
    2.3 Leading   14
    2.4 Controlling   14
    Chapter Summary   15
    Quiz   16

3 Planning and Decision Making   19
    3.1 Define the Problem   20
    3.2 Gather Information   21
    3.3 Identify the Options   21
    3.4 Consider the Data   21
    3.5 Choose an Alternative   22
    3.6 Implement   28
    3.7 Review Your Decision   28
    Chapter Summary   30
    Quiz   31

4 Leaders vs. Managers   35
    4.1 Managerial Traits vs. Leader Traits   36
    4.2 Am I a Manager and a Leader?   38
    Chapter Summary   40
    Quiz   41

5   Organizational Charts and Structure   43

    5.1 Functional   44
    5.2 Divisional   46
    5.3 Matrix   47
    5.4 Team Based   48
    5.5 Network   48
    5.6 Modular   49
    5.7 Organizational Design   50
    Chapter Summary   52
    Quiz   53

6   Budgeting   55

    6.1 Types of Budgets   57
    6.2 Special Budgets   60
    6.3 Other Budgeting Methods   60
    6.4 Budgeting Considerations   61
    Chapter Summary   63
    Quiz   64

7   Problem Solving   67

    7.1 Define the Problem   68
    7.2 Understanding Intricacies   71
    7.3 Processes to Aid in Problem Solving   75
    Chapter Summary   77
    Quiz   78

8   Group Dynamics   81

    8.1 Stages of Group Development   83
    8.2 Group Types   85
    8.3 Factors in Group Behavior   86
    8.4 Causes of Poor Group Dynamics   91
    Chapter Summary   93
    Quiz   95

9 Converting a Group to a Successful Team — 97

9.1 Group vs. Team 98
9.2 Approaches to Improving Team Dynamics 101
Chapter Summary 104
Quiz 105

10 Conflict Resolution — 107

10.1 Types of Conflict 108
10.2 Healthy vs. Unhealthy Conflict Management 109
10.3 Conflict Management Strategies 110
Chapter Summary 116
Quiz 117

11 Communication — 119

11.1 Communication Process 120
11.2 Communication Types 122
11.3 Barriers to Effective Communication 124
11.4 Managerial Communication 126
11.5 General Listening 128
11.6 Active Listening 131
11.7 Tips to Remember about Communication 134
Chapter Summary 136
Quiz 138

12 Change — 141

12.1 Change Management Plan 144
12.2 Change Management Tools 147
Chapter Summary 151
Quiz 152

13 Organizational Culture — 155
13.1 Specific Types of Organizational Culture   156
13.2 Importance of Culture   158
13.3 What Influences Culture?   159
13.4 Disadvantages of Culture   161
13.5 Open Door Policy   162
Chapter Summary   163
Quiz   165

14 Total Quality Management — 167
14.1 Plan   169
14.2 Do   169
14.3 Check   170
14.4 Act   170
14.5 Aspects of TQM   170
14.6 TQM Tools   172
14.7 Production vs. Operations Management   176
Chapter Summary   178
Quiz   179

15 Operations — 181
15.1 Role of Technology   183
Chapter Summary   186
Quiz   187

16 People Management — 189
16.1 Staffing Process   191
16.2 Staffing Challenges   193
16.3 Recruiting Staff   195
16.4 Selecting the Right Employee   197
16.5 Onboarding New Employees   202
16.6 Performance Management   206
Chapter Summary   210
Quiz   211

17 Customer Relationship Management — 215

17.1 Defining Customer Relationship   218
17.2 Types of Customers   219
17.3 Customer Orientation   221
17.4 Ensuring Quality Customer Relationships   222
17.4 Measuring Customer Relationships   224
Chapter Summary   232
Quiz   233

18 International Business and Management — 237

18.1 Why is International Trade Needed?   238
18.2 Forms of Global Business   239
18.3 Domestic vs. International Business: What is the Difference?   241
18.4 Cultural Differences   242
18.5 What type of an International Manager should you be?   245
18.6 How to Choose Where to Expand Internationally   246
Chapter Summary   247
Quiz   249

This page is intentionally left blank

Preface

Many managers will tell you that their first experience with management was the most challenging. Often, employees are recognized for their exemplary performance and are promoted to a manager role. It is assumed that since the employee performed well at their line worker job, they will perform just as well in a management role. What most people do not take into consideration is that the skillset to be a great employee and the skillset to be a great manager are two completely separate things. Some may say they are qualified because they studied it in school but, again, studying and experiencing are two totally different things. So, how do you succeed in this new role of manager knowing that the cards are somewhat stacked against you?

Principles of Management Essentials You Always Wanted To Know seeks to guide you in answering this question. This book consists of core elements of management and being a manager how to support day-to-day activities. New managers may be faced with challenges such as rebuilding a team, developing performance appraisals, dealing with customer complaints, and providing feedback to employees. These items are included in this book along with several other elements to help anyone understand and function in their role of manager. Using real life experiences and detailed study, this book will give you the tools to get started in your management role.

This page is intentionally left blank

Introduction to the book

Management role requires the ability to get things done through teams and individuals. Though managers hold recognized positions of authority in the organization, for a manager to become a leader, he/she needs to develop several qualities and traits.

Management can be effective only if authority, responsibility, and information flow within the organization and are in place. This is possible only if there is a proper organizational structure. With their respective teams, an organization uses time, money, and other resources, effectively and efficiently through budgeting activities. Another activity of importance is problem-solving. This pertains to analyzing a larger problem at hand by understanding its intricacies. This is possible only if the manager is confident in making rational and sound decisions.

This book familiarizes the reader with different levels of authority, leadership effectiveness, managerial effectiveness, decision-making, budgeting, organizational structures, and other functions of management.

While working in an organization, a manager is expected to work with different groups and teams successfully. If a manager is acquainted with group dynamics, it is easier for him/her to handle a team as well as conflicts for the betterment of the organization. A manager should be aware of barriers to effective communication. Therefore, managerial communication is at the core of every effective organization.

Apart from the focus on managerial functions, roles, responsibilities, and challenges, this book elaborately discusses Organizational Culture, Total Quality Management, Operations

Management, People Management, and Customer Relationship Management. This book deals with all such essentials of management and the principles associated with it. In this edition, a new chapter on International Business and Management and quizzes for each chapter are also included.

After going through this book completely, you will be able to:

- Appreciate how the management concepts are built on useful principles that help to achieve any organization's objectives and goals but also facilitate holistic development of all stakeholders.

- Understand that a manager should know the basics of planning, strategizing, organizing, and controlling apart from the techniques of developing and leading a team.

- Accept that, what a manager could achieve through authority accompanying the position in any organization, a leader could achieve by inspiring people.

- Understand the role of organizational charts and structures in achieving the mission of an organization and the impact of organizational culture on the employees and their relationships internally.

- Know that to improve the cohesion of a team, a manager is expected to resolve conflicts cropping up within and outside the team in an organization by adopting various conflict management strategies.

- Understand that communication plays a vital role whenever a change happens in an organization and an effective change management plan prepares the personnel of an organization to successfully sail through the change.

- Appreciate that the largest and most challenging managerial role is in people management
- Understand that Total Quality Management gives every employee a part in the process of ensuring superior products or services.
- Learn the intricacies of International Business and Management as well as the need for expanding the business globally and acquiring the skill set required for the same.

This page is intentionally left blank

Who can benefit from the book?

- Any functional specialist, aspiring for a managerial position to understand and grasp the fundamentals of management concepts quickly.

- Middle and Front line Managers to understand the nuances of various concepts and apply them in their day-to-day work to infuse further quality in their work environment.

- As a reference material to research scholars in management studies.

- Faculty members, professors, and students of management education courses.

How to use this book?

This book provides insights into management principles and acts as a ready reckoner to understand the essential aspects of those principles.

- As the essentials of Management are intertwined, reading the chapters in chronological order will provide a smooth understanding; however checking out a relevant chapter can also be done, as the chapters address the subject matter comprehensively.

- MCQs under each chapter will not only test your understanding but also act as a quick refresher on the topics covered.

This page is intentionally left blank

Chapter 1

Introduction to Management

Management is the process of efficiently and effectively accomplishing organizational tasks and goals with and through other people. This definition of management seems simplistic but the actual performance of the role of management is very complicated. In fact, management is very different from a functional specialist role and can prove to be very challenging. If you strive to succeed and grow in your industry or if you are simply very good at what you do, chances are you will be approached to fill a management role. To be successful as a new manager, you cannot rely on your exceptional technical skills.

Your management toolbox should be filled with knowledge of how to get work accomplished through teams and individuals, planning and strategizing, organizing, controlling, and developing and leading a group as small as a team or as large as an organization. As a manager, you must know how to wear many hats in an organization including negotiator, advocate, mentor, communicator, counselor, conflict resolver, motivator, and so much more. This book is designed to help you build your toolbox and know how and when to wear one of the many hats required.

> Key learning objectives of this chapter include the reader's understanding of the following:
> - Roles and responsibilities of operative level staff to top-level managers
> - Types of authority

1.1 Management Types

Managerial roles are typically housed inside organizations. Organizations are comprised of a group of people brought together to carry out a specific purpose whether it is a for-profit, not-for-profit or government. Organizations across the country and around the world are easily identified by the goals they have set, the structure put into place, and the people involved. An organization's personnel can be categorized as either operatives or managers. Operatives work directly on jobs, tasks, or projects and are not responsible for overseeing the work of others. Managers are more focused on directing the activities of others.

Vertical or top down management defines the level at which an employee is functioning within the organization. Levels include top level managers, middle managers, first-line managers, and operators. The biggest challenge of vertical management is the flow of communication. Two-way communication is difficult to accomplish specifically when lower levels of the organization are trying to communicate up to the top level.

Top-level managers make decisions about where the organization is going and put into place policies that affect all members of the organization. Examples of these managers are the Chief Executive Officer (CEO), Chief Technology Officer (CTO), Chief Financial Officer (CFO), etc. This group of executives are commonly referred to as the "C-suite." Some organizations include their executive vice presidents and division heads as a part of their top management team. These managers are responsible for ensuring long term success for the organization. They pay attention to internal and external environmental drivers when developing long term strategies.

Middle managers exist between the first-line and top levels of management. Examples of these managers are department heads and directors. They act as liaison between the two levels pushing down information to first-line managers and pushing up information to top-level managers. They also take the "big picture" strategic plans developed by the top-level managers and break it down into operational plans for the first-line managers. Middle management's most critical role is implementing directives from the top management team and supporting first-line managers while they work with their teams to complete their day to day activities.

First-line managers direct the day to day activities of employees and are typically entry level roles. Examples of these managers are assistant manager, shift manager, supervisor, office manager, etc. These managers are the closest to the employees and their activities. They are primarily responsible for ensuring organizational plans are completed efficiently and effectively. First-line managers are important because they are usually the first to identify internal issues and problems with operations. For this reason, it is critical that they are communicating frequently with their managers.

1.2 Authority

Authority is the power or right to have others perform the tasks and activities you need them to do. Essentially, authority allows the holder to disperse the organization's resources in a way that will best achieve organizational goals and strategies. There are three main types of authority that can be used in an organization: line, staff, and functional.

Line

Managers have the ability to give employees reporting to them (subordinates) orders or directives. These orders and directives are issued to help efficiently and effectively achieve the organization's goals and objectives. Line authority is given to managers who are directly accountable for departments or areas within the organization to aid them in their required activities. For example, an office manager has line authority over each immediate subordinate according to the organization chart's reporting structure.

Staff

Staff authority is the right to assist or guide those who hold line authority and other employees. Staff authority gives those responsible for performing their tasks the ability to improve effectiveness and efficiency of line employees. Line and staff employees collaborate closely to achieve increased effectiveness and efficiency. For example, supply chain managers have staff authority relative to the office manager. The supply chain manager can advise the office manager on approved items to purchase within the organization.

Functional

Subordinates can veto suggested management directives or propose specific actions based on their area of specialty when they are given functional authority. In many hospitals, physicians are given functional authority to veto management decisions and make recommendations based on their best judgement for patient care.

Chapter Summary

- Management is the process of accomplishing organizational tasks and goals with and through other people effectively and efficiently.

- Vertical, or top-down, management defines the level at which an employee is functioning within the organization and faces the challenge of communication flow especially when the lower level of management is trying to communicate with the top level.

- Top-level managers make decisions about where the organization is going and put into place policies that affect all members of the organization.

- Middle managers are liaisons between top-level and first line managers and are responsible for creating operational plans to achieve the strategic plans of the organizations.

- First-line managers ensure that the organizational plans are completed efficiently and effectively.

- Authority allows management to properly disperse an organization's resources to achieve goals and strategies.

- Line authority is when a manager is assigned to a specific department. They are directly accountable for the performance of these departments.

- ◆ Staff authority oversee those who have line authority and aid in improving efficiency and effectiveness of the line employees.

Quiz

1. To be successful as a manager -

    a. you should have exceptional technical skills

    b. you should sincerely strive to succeed and grow in your field of expertise or domain

    c. your management toolbox should be filled with the knowledge of how to get work accomplished through teams and individuals

    d. you have to work on jobs, tasks, or projects at the operative level for a long period

2. Which of the following statements is wrong?

    a. In the Top-down management hierarchy, the flow of communication from the lower level to the top level is easy to accomplish

    b. Organizations comprise a group of people brought together to carry out a specific purpose irrespective of profit or nonprofit organization

    c. Organizations across the world are identified by the goals set, structure put into place, and people involved

    d. Operatives of organizations are not responsible for overseeing the work of others

3. Which of the following statements is correct?

    a. The managers in C-suite are not responsible for making decisions, formulating policies, and long-term strategies

    b. Paying attention to internal and external environmental drivers and ensuring long-term success for the organization is the responsibility of First-line managers

    c. Implementing directives from Top Management and supporting First-line managers to complete their day-to-day activities are part of the most critical role of department heads and directors

    d. First-line managers are not primarily responsible for ensuring that organizational plans are completed efficiently and effectively

4. Authority allows management to properly disperse an organization's resources to achieve _____

    a. two-way communication

    b. goals and strategies

    c. efficiency and effectiveness

    d. accountability and performance

5. Choose the wrong statement:

   a. Authority is the power or right to have others perform the tasks and activities a manager needs them to do.

   b. Line and Staff employees collaborate closely to achieve increased effectiveness and efficiency.

   c. Line authority is given to managers who are directly accountable for departments or areas within the organization to aid them in their required activities.

   d. Subordinates who are given functional authority, based on their area of specialty are required to abide by management directives; they cannot propose specific actions also.

| **Answers** | 1 – c | 2 – a | 3 – c | 4 – b | 5 – d |

Chapter 2

Functions of Management

In the introduction, we identified management as a process. A process is a group of ongoing and interconnected actions. The management process comprises four main activities: planning, organizing, leading, and controlling. To perform as a successful manager on a day to day basis, you must understand what these functions are and how to differentiate between them.

As we go into the detail of these functions, it is important to know management functions are not always linear. As a manager, you may encounter an unplanned problem or issue. In that case, you may begin at the organizing part of the process or controlling part of the process rather than at the planning phase. As you begin to address the issue, unforeseen items will come up which will cause you to move to another part of the process. As a manager, you should be able to identify what functions to implement and ensure the integrity of the management process is maintained.

> Key learning objectives of this chapter include the reader's understanding of the following:
> - Planning
> - Organizing
> - Leading
> - Controlling

Figure 2.1

2.1 Planning

Planning is a formal process managers follow to choose goals, identify next steps, allocate resources to complete the steps, measure how successful they were in completing the steps and then revisiting plans to determine how they can improve upon the process and steps in the future. Planning includes developing overall strategies for the organization. It goes a step further than strategy development and includes regulation of a wide variety of activities in an organization.

A strategy or strategic plan affects the entire organization and is typically long-term. The strategic plan outlines where the organization is currently and where it wishes to be. Tactical plans further breakdown strategic plans into specific activities the organization needs to implement. The tactical plans detail the activities to be completed, who will be responsible for their completion, and what is needed for successful completion.

2.2 Organizing

When planning is completed, we need to determine what the best way is to implement. When organizing, you are determining the most appropriate organizational structure for the plan implementation. Examples of this structure may include organizing by departments, matrix teams, project teams, etc. This function is also used to assign authority and responsibility to appropriate teams or departments, defining resource allocation, and detailing how the tasks will be organized. Reporting relationships and decision-making structure is defined during the organizing function as well.

2.3 Leading

Leading is arguably the most important of the four management functions. The best plans cannot be executed without people to support the plan and complete the tasks. Leaders are placed in organizations to motivate employees and inspire teams to achieve their goals. Leaders create enthusiasm, communicate through all levels of the organization, encourage high performance, and create a commitment among employees to a shared vision, values, and culture. Leaders are also responsible for less popular tasks such as resolving conflicts, taking disciplinary actions, and implementing decisions that are not well supported amongst employees.

2.4 Controlling

The controlling function is often an ongoing activity and a critical one too. It is the process of monitoring performance, measuring it against baselines and goals, and implementing interventions where necessary. It is where we get the information to report whether we are performing well according to our goals and essentially implementing our strategies. Continuous review of these activities helps the organization to stay on track to accomplishing the strategic plan.

Chapter Summary

- The four functions of management are planning, organizing, leading, and controlling.

- Planning leads managers to developing an overall strategy by selecting goals, next steps, allocating resources, determining success rates, and revisiting plans to improve the overall strategy in the future.

- Organizing determines the organizational structure for executing the plan, assigns authority, defines resource allocations and details how tasks will be organized.

- Leading identifies those who will head the execution of the plan and manage all tasks during implementation. It involves motivating the employees and inspiring the teams to achieve their goals.

- Controlling is an ongoing activity of monitoring the performance of the plan, comparing it to the baseline or goals, and implementing interventions where necessary.

Quiz

1. Which of the following is the most important management function?

    a. Planning

    b. Organizing

    c. Leading

    d. Controlling

2. Which of the following statements is not correct?

    a. Management functions are always linear

    b. While engaged in addressing an issue, unforeseen items will come up which will cause the manager to move to another part of the process

    c. As a manager, when you encounter an unplanned problem, you can address it in the organizing phase or controlling phase rather than the planning phase

    d. A manager should ensure the integrity of the management process being maintained and identify what functions to implement

3. Which of the following options fulfills the following three criteria?
   i. This affects the entire organization for a long term;
   ii. This includes regulation of a wide variety of activities in an organization;
   iii. This outlines where the organization is currently and where it wishes to be.
   a. Tactical plan
   b. Organizational structure
   c. Strategic plan
   d. Monitoring performance

4. Identify the wrong statement:
   a. The most appropriate organizational structure for plan implementation is determined at the Organizing stage
   b. Organizing function is used to assign authority and responsibility to appropriate teams or departments, define resource allocation, and describe how the task will be organized
   c. Reporting relationships and decision-making structures are defined while organizing
   d. Breakdown of strategic plans into specific activities needs to be implemented during the organizing stage

5. Which of the following is true about the leadership function?

   a. It is an ongoing activity and a critical function

   b. Monitoring performance, measuring it against baselines and goals, and implementing interventions, wherever necessary

   c. To get information on whether we are performing well according to our goals and essentially implementing our strategies

   d. To communicate through all levels of the organization, encourage high performance, and create a commitment among employees to a shared vision, values, and culture

| **Answers** | 1 – c | 2 – a | 3 – c | 4 – d | 5 – d |

Chapter 3

Planning and Decision Making

One of the most important things you will do as a manager is make decisions. It is a primary function of management that should be done carefully in order to make rational and sound decisions. A decision is a choice made between different courses of action in circumstances of ambiguity to best achieve the desired outcome or objective. Decision making is a thought process of selecting the best choice from the available possibilities. This process includes considering the positives and negatives of each option and consideration of all alternatives to forecast the possible outcomes.

Key learning objectives of this chapter include the reader's understanding of the following:

- Steps involved in decision making
- Different types of decision-making techniques

- Importance of Heuristic approaches
- Implementation and review of the decisions made

Recommended steps for making a thoughtful decision include:
- Defining the problem or the decision to be made
- Gathering information and collecting data
- Identifying the options and possibilities
- Considering the data
- Choosing an alternative
- Implementing the alternative
- Reviewing the decision made and evaluating the consequences.

3.1 Define the Problem

Make sure to clearly detail and document the problem or decision that needs to be made. Clearly defining what needs to be addressed is crucial to success.

3.2 Gather Information

Gather information from various sources pertaining to the decision. What is the current state of the issue? What do you want the future state to look like? Determine what information you need, where is the best place to get it, and how you will obtain the information.

3.3 Identify the Options

While sorting through the information gathered, various options and alternatives will become evident. Document those options and use those options to create new ones. Listing all feasible alternatives is critical in coming to an informed decision.

3.4 Consider the Data

Examine each of the possibilities you have outlined and weigh the pros and cons. Forecast what the outcome may look like should you choose a particular option. Is the outcome desirable? Does it align with organizational goals and objectives? Will the problem really be resolved? After completing this process, you can take the list of options and rank them to show the best options.

3.5 Choose an Alternative

Now that you have completed a thorough analysis, you can make an informed decision based on your list of priorities.

Decision Making Techniques

A decision is the outcome of the decision-making process. What are some techniques commonly used for making decisions? Let's start by understanding the difference between a programmed and a non-programmed decision.

A programmed decision-process deals best with recurring issues. An organization should strive to handle recurring issues in a consistent manner. It does this by having well-defined decision rules in place normally documented as policies and procedures. This will result in maximum efficiency and least risk to the organization. Each transaction or problem does not have to be dealt with on a "one-off" basis, conserving personnel's time and energy. This can be especially important as senior management will not need to be involved in the day-by-day operation of the business. Training personnel to handle similar issues or problems in a consistent way is also critical.

Examples of programmed decisions are: (i) what to do if an employee is consistently late for work; (ii) how to handle daily transactions in the accounting department; and (iii) hospital emergency room procedures. Personnel dealing with the above activities should not deviate from previously defined standard procedures. You would not want the human resources director to treat people differently in identical circumstances. Not only is this patently unfair, but it could expose the organization to potential litigation. Similarly, you don't want accounting department personnel dealing with routine transactions on an ad hoc basis. One goal of good financial accounting is consistency. And of course, you definitely don't want hospitals to lack procedures in the emergency room, as human lives can be stake.

What makes all of these decisions similar is they can be programmed. They are recurring, can be systematized and be efficiently dealt with in that manner. Sometimes programmed decision making is dictated from external authorities. For instance, financial accounting departments are required by regulators and professional ethics to maintain adequate internal controls. It is not an option. A good system of internal controls requires consistency of treatment and adequate documentation of each transaction, a prototypical example of programmed decision-making.

Critics may claim this is a bureaucratic way (in the worst sense of the word) of handling decision-making. Programmed decision-making challenges management in many ways:

- Personnel must know when to "kick" decisions upstairs and do so without fear. They need to understand their jobs well enough to know when they should not attempt to make decisions on their own. Adequate training is critical for successful implementation of a programmed decision-making process.

- There still must be opportunities to innovate within the system. Programmed decision processes must not be allowed to ossify over time. Employees are often the best source of suggested improvement in any process. Employee suggestion boxes, bonuses for improvement suggestions, productivity awards etc. are a few simple techniques to help the organization to innovate.

- Management should never set up a programmed decision-making process and then simply leave it alone. The process must be monitored and reevaluated on a continuous basis. Supervisors should always be alert for the opportunity to improve the decision-making process. Technological advances such as artificial intelligence and robotic process automation need to be factored into the programmed decision process as they become available.

- The programmed decision-process must be sensitive to the needs of customers. Efficient decision-making is of no value if customers are alienated. Again, training can go a long way to address this particular concern. Customer service awards can also be offered on a regular basis.

Non-programmed decisions are usually made in response to unique, poorly defined, or unstructured issues, including classic "one-off" situations. Non-programmed decisions often have the largest impact on an organization. A famous example of non-programmed decision-making is the way Johnson & Johnson ("J&J") handled the Tylenol poisonings in the 1980s. Someone was introducing poison into Tylenol, a common pain reliever made by J & J. Seven people died as a result of the drug-tampering. J & J used multiple taskforces to quickly counter the escalating problem. It recalled all Tylenol products and introduced new tamper-proof packaging. This was done at enormous cost as Tylenol was one of J & J's major product lines. Management's swift and effective decision-making earned the accolades of everyone. Within a short time, Tylenol was back on the market and was once again a successful product for J & J.

Which is the preferred method of decision-making? Programmed decision-making and nonprogrammed decision-making are complimentary. No one wants to waste a lot of time dealing with recurring activities. On the other hand, a challenge can be so novel the decision-making processes in place can get overwhelmed and become inadequate for the job. This is when non-programmed decision-making comes into play.

Smaller non-programmed decisions can be made with the use of heuristics. A heuristic can be best thought of as a decision rule. Decisions having a small return and small risk but need to be made are often handled through a heuristic decision-making process. Dealing with each problem with exacting analysis results in organizational "paralysis by analysis". Heuristics help eliminate this problem. Examples of low-risk and low return non-programmed decision-making are: (i) what color should the office be painted; (ii) how should office space be divided; and (iii) how to assign reserved parking spaces. None of these decisions have a large return or a large risk, but yet they need to be made quickly.

Let's demonstrate how several well-known heuristic rules would work on a common office problem. Suppose the lease on the office copier is about to expire after three years. New models with new features have been introduced into the market.

Three copier companies have been asked to demonstrate their products. How should management go about picking out the new copier?

Let's look at a few decision rules:

- **The recognition heuristic.**—You know very little about copiers and copier brands. After evaluating the copiers, you are still undecided about which to buy. Of the three, you recognize one copier company as nationally known for its product quality. Since you recognize this company, you lease their copier. This heuristic works well when quality is correctly associated with the product brand. This is one-reason why companies pour so much money into advertising.

- **"What did we do last time?"** — This methodology works extremely well when a lot of time and effort had been previously expended on the same issue. In the case of the copier, perhaps an exhaustive study had been done the last time a copier needed to be purchased. Rather than repeat the study again, the decision is based on the previous analysis. The decision-maker must take care to see any new information critical to the decision be reviewed. For example, the new copier might also need to serve as a printer and a document scanner. These features may not have been factored into the last decision.

- **Lexicographic strategies.** — A lexicographic decision-making strategy involves ranking attributes. The decision is made based on the most important attribute. If there is a tie on the most important attribute, the next most important attribute is considered. In our copier case, the most important attribute to the purchaser might be price. The second most important attribute might be service. The cheaper copier would be purchased based on these decision rules. In the unlikely event the copiers are the same price, the service contract would then be considered. A semi-lexicographic strategy is a little more flexible. If allows for the successive attributes to be considered if the most important attribute of the three copiers are similarly rated. Suppose the difference in price between the three copiers is no more than $10 per month. This is deemed to be inconsequential to the decision-maker so the next attribute would be examined and so on until a decision is made.

- **Elimination by aspects.** —The decision maker sets certain criteria that need to be met. Sample criteria could be: (i) the copier should not cost more than $10,000 per year; (II) It must do color-copying, and (iii) service must be guaranteed to arrive in less than twenty-four hours. The copier selected must conform to all of these specifications.

- **Satisficing.** —Options will continue to be reviewed sequentially until a satisfactory alternative is obtained. Suppose the second copier reviewed by the decision maker has all of the attributes needed. The decision maker will not invite the third salesmen in, as the decision to buy the second copier determined. Satisficing does not guarantee the optimal copier purchase, but simply a satisfactory one.

How robust are heuristics in decision-making? Decision makers typically can only devote a small amount of time to these types of decisions. The consequences of a wrong decision are not steep as the risk and rewards are limited. Indeed, it is critical managers devote sufficient attention to decisions with wider repercussions, and heuristics provide a way to deal with smaller decisions quickly. How many times have you heard the following in an office setting: "We spend more time deciding who will get what office than we do on our strategic plan?" A heuristic rule could quickly dispose of the office allocation problem. This is not to say that who gets what office is not an important decision, but certainly any manager should want to spend more time on strategic decisions.

What about more complex decisions having higher risk and higher return? Much more time is warranted in studying these decisions. Some techniques involved in these decisions are probability analysis, Monte Carlo simulation, simple multi-attribute rating techniques (SMART) and others. These advanced techniques are covered in another book in this series.

3.6 Implement

Take the final decision and determine what you will need to do to implement it. Then, allocate the appropriate resources and complete the tasks to make the decision operational.

3.7 Review Your Decision

The decision-making process does not stop at implementation. It is vital you observe how the implemented decision is performing and whether your desired objective is being met. Determine how you will measure success and compare the results to where you want to be. Is the process working? Are there any issues coming up? Take the time to address interventions to address any issues and measure again.

Decision making can be done by an individual or by a group. Individual decision making can save time, money and energy because people tend to make prompt decisions. Group decisions tend to take a longer time which costs money and energy.

Individuals can also be held accountable for their decisions made whereas accountability is a little more difficult to pin down in a group. Groups can collect more information and with the points of view of several members, is not biased by one individual. Groups can also take into consideration effects of a decision on different areas of the company whereas an individual decision-maker may have a more limited view.

Chapter Summary

- ◆ A decision is a choice between different courses of action and should be carefully thought out using the following steps:

    - Define the problem or decision to be made

    - Gather information and collect data

    - Identify the options and possibilities

    - Consider the data

    - Choose an alternative

    - Implement

    - Review the decisions made and evaluate any good or bad consequences

Quiz

1. Which of the following statement is wrong? Decision-making is a _____

   a. primary function of Management

   b. thought process of selecting the best choice

   c. process of considering positives and negatives of each option

   d. choice made in circumstances of clarity to best achieve the desired objective

2. Steps of the decision-making process are given below; which of the following options are in the right order?

   i. Gather information from various sources

   ii. Detail and document the problem

   iii. List out all feasible alternatives from the information

   iv. Weigh the pros and cons of the possibilities

   a. (i → ii → iii → iv)

   b. (ii → i → iii → iv)

   c. (iii → iv → ii → i)

   d. (iv → iii → ii → i)

3. Which of the following is not acceptable about group decision-making?

   a. Can save time, money, and energy

   b. Tends to take a longer time, more money, or energy

   c. Accountability is relatively difficult to pin down

   d. Group can collect more information

4. This strategy involves ranking attributes. The decision is based on the most important attribute. It is called a _____ strategy

   a. Elimination by aspect

   b. Satisficing

   c. Lexicographic

   d. 'What did we do last time'

5. Heuristics are not applicable for which of the following:

   a. What color should the office be painted?

   b. What to do if an employee is consistently late for work?

   c. How should office space be divided?

   d. How to assign reserved parking spaces?

6. Which of the following is not true?

   a. Programmed and non-programmed decision-making are complimentary

   b. Smaller non-programmed decisions cannot be made with heuristics

   c. Non-programmed decisions can be made to unique, poorly defined 'one off' situations.

   d. A good system of internal controls with the consistency of treatment and adequate documentation of each transaction is an example of programmed decision making

| **Answers** | 1 – d | 2 – b | 3 – b | 4 – c | 5 – b | 6 – b |

This page is intentionally left blank

Chapter 4

Leaders vs. Managers

The words "leaders" and "managers" are often used synonymously, but they actually have different meanings. The primary difference between management and leadership is managers hold recognized positions of authority in the organizational structure where leaders may not. A leader can be anyone in an organization, but they do frequently hold managerial positions. As you may have encountered, not all managers may qualify as good leaders. When this happens, people tend to follow orders not because they are motivated to but because they are obliged to.

Managers with line authority can compel employees to follow their directives. Integral to their role is the ability to judge employee performance, and to promote, reward, correct, hire or fire employees accordingly.

People do not follow leaders because they are compelled by formal authority from the organization. They follow them because they feel moved to do so. People choose to follow a leader due to the leader's personality, principles, and behaviors. Leaders are passionate about their work and as a result of that, they dive into their work full force. They care about others, especially those who follow them. They want others to feel the passion they do, so they invest their time into helping others be successful and satisfied in their work. Leaders aren't strictly focused on organizational goals and objectives.

> Key learning objectives of this chapter include the reader's understanding of the following:
>
> - Difference between leadership and management in terms of the impact of formal authority
> - The reason why people follow a manager's directive and the reasons for following a leader
> - How the traits of a leader differ from that of a Manager
> - Different tests to decide whether you are a leader or a manager

4.1 Managerial Traits vs. Leader Traits

One way to distinguish between a manager and a leader is by their personal traits. Below are important traits of both managers and leaders.

Traits a manager possesses are:

- **Vision for the future** — Using a roadmap for his or her team to follow, a manager successfully implements a strategic vision.

- **A talent for directing** — Anticipating needs and course correcting where needed on a day to day basis is critical to a manager's success.

- **An ability to manage processes** — With their role, managers have the authority to implement rules, standards, procedures, and processes.

- **Engaging and people centric** — In order to build the trust, loyalty, and productivity of employees, managers stay up to date on their employees' needs and if they are being met. To do this, managers must practice active listening, engage employees in critical decisions, and make every effort to meet any sensible requests for changes.

Traits a leader possesses are:

- **An ability to see the big picture** — Leaders see the forest for the trees. They know where they are going and how to get there from where they currently are. They engage others to help them identify the course of action to take to get to their desired state.

- **Trustworthiness and reliability** — People follow leaders because they are honest and have integrity. Believing in this leader motivates others to journey down the path the leader lays out.

- **Stimulation** — Leaders can stimulate or inspire others to see how their day to day work affects the bigger picture.

- **Communication skills** — Leaders communicate well and often so that their team knows the current happenings, future endeavors, and possible hurdles in the future.

- **Ability to issue a challenge** — Leaders are not afraid to challenge anything needing change. They are "outside the box" thinkers who have their own way of doing things.

4.2 Am I a Manager and a Leader?

How do you know if you are inspiring others to follow rather than ordering them to? Vineet Nayar details three different tests that can be used in the article, Three Differences Between Managers and Leaders.

- **Calculating value vs. Generating Value** — Since managers are heavily focused on meeting organizational goals and objectives, they tend to count or calculate value rather than try to create it. Leaders are free of this obligation, therefore they put their energies into creating value.

- **Circles of influence vs. Circles of Power** — Subordinates required to follow direction create a circle of power for a manager. Leaders have motivated followers who create a circle of influence. Do people outside of your reporting relationship seek guidance from you? If your answer is yes, then you are a leader.

- **Leading People vs. Managing People** — Managers control employees with their organizational authority or power given to them in order to meet goals and objectives. Leaders inspire, motivate, encourage and enable others to give back to the organization without control or power.

Chapter Summary

- The difference between leadership and management is that management is a recognized position of authority, and leadership can be identified within any employee whether they are a manager.

- People follow managers because they are obligated to, and leaders because they are motivated to.

- Managers poses traits such as accomplishing a vision, a talent for directing, ability to manage processes, and are people centric.

- Leaders possess traits such as the ability to see the big picture, trustworthiness and reliability, stimulation, communication skills, and the ability to issue a challenge.

Quiz

1. **Which of the following is true?**

    a. People follow the directive of managers out of their own willingness and motivation they get.

    b. Leaders always hold recognized positions of authority in an organization.

    c. All managers may not qualify as good leaders.

    d. Managers with Line authority cannot compel employees to follow their directives.

2. **Which of the following is a managerial trait?**

    a. An ability to see the big picture

    b. Stimulating qualities

    c. Communication skills

    d. People-centric

3. **Which of the following is not a leadership trait?**

    a. Ability to issue a challenge

    b. Inspiring qualities

    c. Communication skills

    d. Accomplishing a strategic vision

4. Which of the following is not true?

   a. Anticipating needs on a day-to-day basis is critical to a manager's success

   b. A manager motivates others to tread on the path they lay out

   c. Managers stay up to date on their employee's needs and whether they are being fulfilled

   d. Leaders communicate well to equip their team about current happenings, future endeavors, and possible hurdles in the future

5. Which one is not a test prescribed by Vineet Nayar to find out whether you are a manager or a leader?

   a. Calculating Value vs. Generating Value

   b. Ability to manage processes vs. Stimulation

   c. Circles of Influence vs. Circles of Power

   d. Leading People vs. Managing People

| Answers | 1 – c | 2 – d | 3 – d | 4 – b | 5 – b |

Chapter 5

Organizational Charts and Structure

An organizational chart is a picture or diagram of how authority, responsibility, and information flow within the formal organization structure. The chart shows the structure of the organization and the relationships between its parts down to ranks of positions and jobs. Organizational structure is comprised of an organization of tasks, reporting associations, and an organization of communications linking people and positions. Essentially, structures show how labor is divided amongst employees and detail people or groups performing different roles in the organization. Formal structures are detailed in the official organization chart. Informal structures show unofficial relationships that are developed amongst organization employees. Structures that allow people and groups to work effectively and efficiently together are ideal.

> Key learning objectives of this chapter include the reader's understanding of the following:
>
> - Different roles of people or groups in the organization
> - Advantages and disadvantages of six different types of structures, namely Functional, Divisional, Matrix, Team-based, Network, and Modular.
> - Changes in the organizational designs with trends in the industry

There are six types of structures that can be reflected in an organizational chart:

- Functional
- Divisional
- Matrix
- Team Based
- Network Structure
- Modular

5.1 Functional

People with similar tasks or responsibilities are assembled into a functional structure. This structure is one of the more common in organizations and it fosters quick decision making because the decision makers are easily able to communicate with one another. Another advantage is people can learn new things from each other because they have similar skill sets and interests. A disadvantage of this structure is functional groups may create silos and not communicate outside of their functional group affecting creativity and innovation. An example of a functional structure would be an Information Technology department that has a hardware team specifically responsible for computer hardware.

Figure 5.1

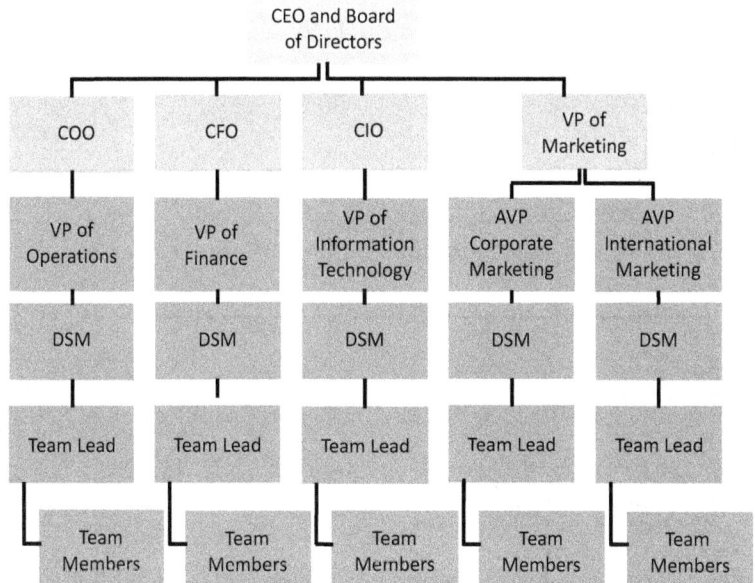

5.2 Divisional

A work team is created to foster inter-group relationships to meet the needs of the customer in a divisional structure. This structure allows for better production of varieties of similar products. A divisional structure is desirable when issues in one division do not directly affect the other divisions. Separating out into specialized functions can result in operational inefficiencies, a potential disadvantage of this structure. Divisions that are set up geographically, grouping employees into regions to work with each other producing similar products for a specific region is an example of divisional structure.

Figure 5.2

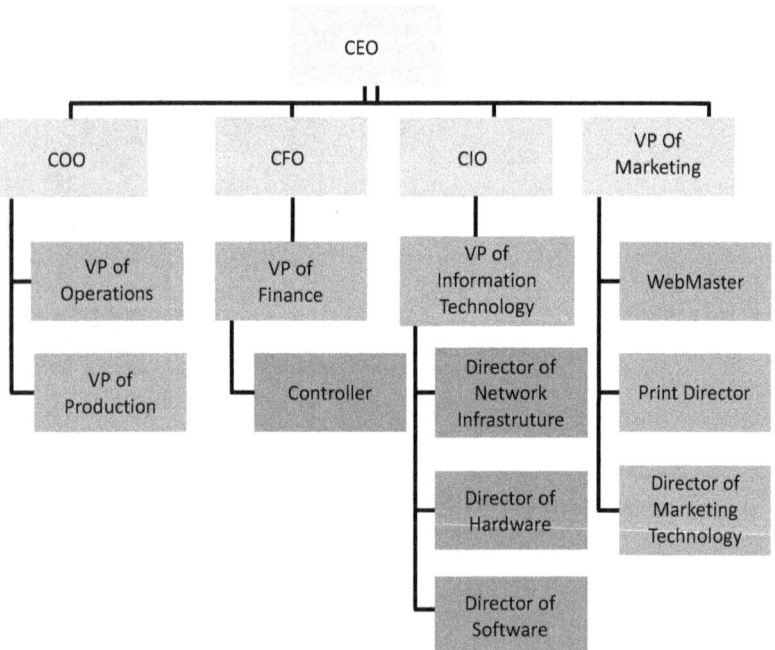

5.3 Matrix

One of the more complex structures is the matrix structure. It is complex because it groups people in two ways, by role performed and by the product group they work with. This structure gives team members more responsibility and ability to work independently. A benefit of this structure is increased productivity of the team, increased inventiveness, and ability to make decisions through group collaboration. It also creates a complicated chain of command, possibly conflicting with employees due to competing loyalties. You may see a matrix structure when special projects are being implemented in an organization.

Figure 5.3

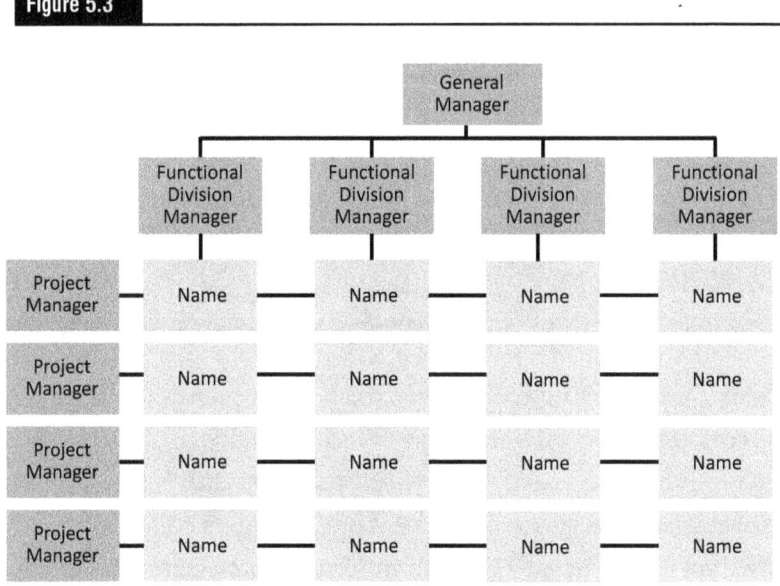

5.4 Team Based

This structure is a new type you may see in larger organizations. The team consists of a group of employees with matched skills and synergistic efforts accomplishing a common objective. Cross-functional teams are people grouped together from different functions in the organization.

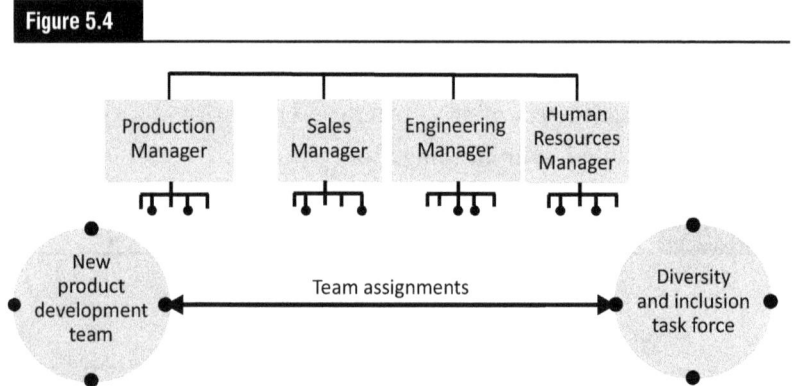

Figure 5.4

5.5 Network

Another emerging type of organizational structure is the network structure. This structure is less hierarchical, decentralized and has more operational flexibility. Social network is the main concept this structure is based on. Managers create social networks with open lines of communication between both internal and external partners. The structure's main advantage is agility. The network has fewer layers of management due to the decentralization and a wider area of control. The bottom-up flow of ideas and decisions is encouraged. The downside to this structure is it can result in more complexity within the relations in the organization. As technology has advanced, virtual organizations have begun to develop in network structures. Virtual organizations depend on information technology to link groups and essential services.

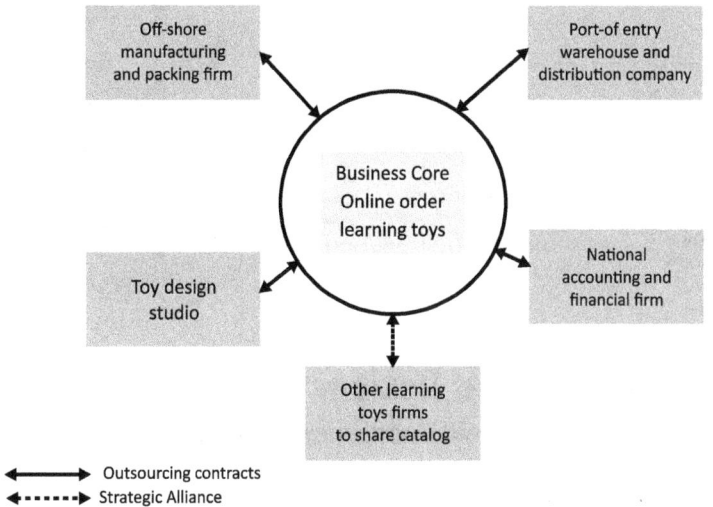

Figure 5.5

5.6 Modular

Businesses are divided into small, strategic business units (SBUs) that place their emphasis on specific parts of the organizational process. There are few interdependencies between SBUs and there is great flexibility. Since the structure is loosely constructed, organizations can be more flexible and restructure more easily in a modular structure. Critics of this structure argue the number of SBUs can affect communication and intellectual property gains. They recommend limiting the modules to reduce flexibility so better gains can be produced.

Figure 5.6

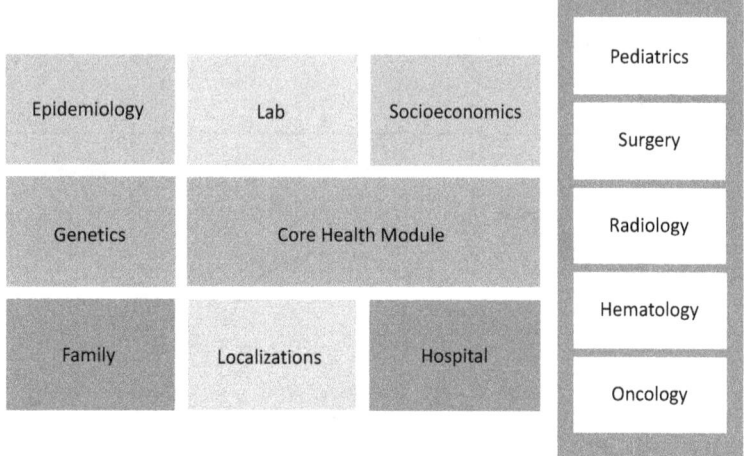

5.7 Organizational Design

The purpose of organizational design is to create an organizational structure designed to best achieve the mission and of the organization and respond to external drivers. Organizational designs are always changing with trends in the industry and growing technology. As new studies come out about how people work and relate to one another, organizations modify their organizational design to what is most appropriate for the organization.

Some trends we are currently seeing is a flatter structure where there are fewer layers of management. This is referred to as span of control. A narrow span of control is where the manager supervises few people. A wide span of control is where the manager supervises a large number of people. With the emerging trend of flatter organizations, you tend to see a wider span of control.

Organizations are branching out and becoming more decentralized. If the organization remains centralized, top management retains control over decision making. As we are seeing now with increased decentralization, decision making is actually dispersed throughout an organization.

More delegation and empowerment of employees is greatly encouraged in today's business environment. Employees are given the right to make decisions and take action more autonomously. Once decision making rights are granted to the employee, they can act as needed to accomplish the task and are held accountable for completing the task.

Flexibility is key with organizational design today, so you are seeing more horizontal organizations able to adapt to changes quickly. The designs are typically organic and decentralized. There are few rules and procedures, wide span of control, shared tasks, information coordination and many teams. This is as opposed to the traditional design which has more bureaucracy with formal authority dictating rules to ensure order and fairness. In this structure there are many rules, narrow span of control, specialized tasks, formal coordination, and few teams.

Due to advancements in technology, needs of the workforce, and the need for cost reduction, organizations are considering more alternative work schedules. Making this change has increased satisfaction of both the employer and employees. Examples of alternative work schedules are a compressed work week, flextime, job sharing, and telecommuting.

Chapter Summary

- There are six types of organizational structures that lead to an organization achieving their mission and responding to external drivers.

- Functional is most common, allows quick decision making, and considers employees with similar tasks and responsibilities.

- Divisional fosters inter-group relationships focusing on customer needs and improves production but can lead to operational inefficiencies.

- Matrix groups people by role performed and product group, increases productivity, inventiveness and ability to make decisions through group interactions.

- Team based consists of a group with matched skills and common objectives.

- Network has fewer layers due to decentralizations, a wider area of control, bottom-up flow of ideas and decisions, but relationships within the organization become more complex.

- Modular focuses on strategic business units and allows great flexibility, however, too many SBUs can lead to a lack in communication and intellectual property gains.

- Organizational Design - Designing the organizational structure to best achieve the goals of the organization and respond to external drivers.

- Current trends indicate a flatter structure where there are fewer layers of management. Flexibility is key with organization design.

Quiz

1. Which of the following is not applicable regarding the organization chart?

    a. It is a picture of authority, responsibility, and information flow within the formal organizational structure

    b. There are 6 types of structures that can be reflected by the organization chart

    c. Informal structures are detailed in the organization chart

    d. The chart shows the relationships between its parts down to ranks of positions and jobs of an organization

2. Which of the following describes functional structure?

    a. This is common in organizations and fosters quick decision-making

    b. People learn new things from each other

    c. It results in silos as members do not communicate outside their functional group

    d. All of the above

3. Which of the following is/are applicable to the divisional structure?

    a. Separating out into specialized functions can result in operational inefficiencies

    b. To foster intergroup relationships to meet the needs of the customer, a work team is created

c. It is desirable when issues in one division do not affect the other division directly

d. All of the above

4. Which of the following is/are the advantages of a Matrix structure?

   a. It creates a complicated chain of command

   b. It gives team members more responsibility and the ability to work independently

   c. Increased productivity and increased inventiveness

   d. Options b and c

5. Which of the following is not true about a Team based structure?

   a. This is followed in smaller organizations only

   b. A team consists of employees with matching skills

   c. Team members' synergistic efforts help to achieve common objectives

   d. Cross-functional teams are grouped together from different functions

| **Answers** | 1 – c | 2 – d | 3 – d | 4 – d | 5 – a |

Chapter 6

Budgeting

Another critical activity of a manager is budgeting. Time and money are valuable commodities in an organization. Managers must use their resources efficiently and effectively to get the value-add. Managers use a budget to plan and control optimal use of the resources. Details of the organization's objectives and how to obtain the resources to meet those objectives are also in the budget plan.

Key learning objectives of this chapter include the reader's understanding of the following:

- Importance of budgeting
- Different types of budgets such as sales budget, production budget, manufacturing cost center budget, cash budget, and special budgets
- Budgeting methods and considerations for budgeting

Budgeting is typically used as a planning and controlling system for financial aspects of the organization. Referencing the management process, we discussed earlier, let's walk through the budgeting process. The first step of budgeting is planning. Management develops various types of budgets into an implementation plan. Management works with their teams to operationally implement the budget plans they created. Typically, these plans include possible changes to daily operations and staffing. In the next step, management controls the implementation of this plan by observing the outcomes of what has been implemented, measuring them against objectives, and applying interventions appropriately.

The planning process in budgeting focuses on what may happen in the future. The plan identifies what we want to do and what internal and external variables may come into play. First, the goal must be identified in the budget plan to answer the question "What do we want to accomplish?" Goals can be set terms of profit, market share, cost containment, maintaining market position, or expanding product lines.

Next, performance objectives are identified. These objectives are sub-goals that will help us meet our overall objectives. They give us a way to monitor our progress on a regular basis so that we can update our forecasts regularly to determine if we will meet the goals and objectives we identified. For example, XYZ Organization set a goal to increase market share by 30% so it set a sub-goal to increase its Hispanic and senior customer base by 15% each. Performance objectives can be broken down even further as you trickle the goal down into the organization. To build on this example, the marketing department decided to set a goal of running three marketing campaigns targeting seniors during the year to reach the larger performance objective.

In summary, budgeting is completed to forecast spending and income, aid in decision making, and measure how the organization is performing.

6.1 Types of Budgets

In general, when referring to budgeting, managers may refer to a master budget, planned operating budget, or a financial budget. The master budget is simply the planned operating budget and the financial budget. The planned operating budget aids in future planning of income and produces a projected income statement. The financial budget allows management to plan on how they will finance assets and produces a projected balance sheet.

Coordination of the budget plans of all the departments in the organization are critical to the success of meeting the organization's financial goals and objectives. These goals and objectives should be integrated and coordinated amongst all areas to ensure achievement. This coordination is typically accomplished through various areas creating different types of budgets and plans. The flow of the budget preparation in the traditional budgeting method is detailed below:

- The strategic and long-range plan is developed by higher level management and executives to guide the overall objectives and goals.

- The long-range sales forecast and the capital expenditure budgets are created from this plan. The long-range sales forecast estimates the sales needed in the future to meet

www.vibrantpublishers.com

the strategic goals. The capital expenditure budgets detail what funds and resources will be utilized to obtain physical assets that will help meet the organization goals.

- The sales budget is the first budget to be created. This budget shows estimated sales in a specified time period and the estimated price per item. It also shows the overall estimated total of sales.

Sales budget
Budgeted sales revenue = budgeted sales unit X budgeted sales price

- The information in the sales budget is often used to aid in developing the marketing expense budget and the production budget. The marketing expense budget details an estimate of how much it would cost to sell the amount of products identified in the sales budget.

- The production budget shows how much of the product needs to be manufactured in order to sell the amount of product in the sales budget.

Production budget
Budgeted sales units + desired finished product inventory – beginning finished goods inventory = units to be produced

- The production budget influences the inventory budget and the manufacturing cost center budgets. The inventory budget defines the cost of any finished products we have on hand in a given time period. Essentially, the inventory budget describes what it costs us to have this product on hand and not sold?

- The manufacturing cost center budget looks at three sub-budgets for each cost center (or area) to forecast how much direct materials will cost, what labor may cost, and overhead predict for the amount of product produced. The manufacturing cost center budget also provides input to the profit plan and back to the inventory budget.

Manufacturing Cost Center Budget
Direct material cost per unit = materials required per unit X material cost per unit

Direct labor cost per unit = direct labor required per unit X labor rate per hour

Overhead per unit = total overhead cost with depreciation/units to be produced

- The profit plan details the steps you will take to meet the goal profit level. The profit plan influences the cash budget.

- The cash budget is a forecast of the inflow and outflow of cash for a specified period of time. With this forecast, managers can tell if their area has enough cash to operate. The capital expenditure budget discussed in point b) also contributes to the cash budget.

Cash budget
Total cash collections – payments for purchases – other cash payments = excess of collections over payments

Excess of collections over payments + beginning cash balance = ending cash balance

- The balance sheet budget is created from the cash budget and capital expenditure budgets. This budget consists of everything you would normally see in a balance sheet except it is a forecast of what the balance sheet may look like in future time periods.

6.2 Special Budgets

One budget not mentioned in this process is a flexible operating budget. This budget details the budgeted expenses and revenues at different levels of output. Flexible budgets are good because we can look at the budget in relation to the actual level of output. This would give us a more accurate picture when we compare the flexible budget to our actuals. When we compare the actual level of activity, variances in volume are not an issue so management can look at cost variances only.

For the same level of operations, the difference between the actual costs and the flexible budget is referred to as the budget variance. Budget variances are a great tool to use to see how efficiently you are performing. Budget variances can be reviewed for every line item in the budget using the performance report.

6.3 Other Budgeting Methods

Another method of budgeting is zero based budgeting. Managers start their budgets at zero and then have to justify every dollar placed in the budget. A lot of paperwork goes into this method where managers document the activities of their area and why it is important that they get funding for each activity. This information is placed into a decision packet and sent to higher level managers for approval. The biggest disadvantage of this method is the time consumed creating the paperwork for decision making.

6.4 Budgeting Considerations

Creating the actual budgets and plans are the first part of the process. The budgets and plans have to be implemented. In order to be implemented most effectively, the following conditions should be in place:

- **Top management support** — All levels of management, from executive to front line, should know the importance of the budget to the company and meeting the company's objectives. The overall organization goals and objectives should be communicated throughout the organization so that all employees understand how budgets can be affected by their actions.

- **Collaborative goal setting** — Budgets are most effective when everyone has a stake in what has been decided. Participatory budgeting is when all managers having a stake in the decision have input into the budget. If you take this concept down a level in the organization, managers can include their employees in preparing and setting their budgets, so they have buy-in from their team. Including their employees will also assist in improving the accuracy of the budget since employees often have more detailed and helpful information than the managers.

- **Communicating results** — Discussion of the budget, budget progress, and issues should be held often. All team members should understand the current state of the budget so they can make any changes accordingly.

- **Flexibility** — Be sure to state any assumptions for the budget as accompanying documentation. If anything changes during the time period, update those assumptions and budgets accordingly. Making these changes gives us an up to date view of how we are performing to budget.

- **Follow-up** — Follow-up on the budget and any feedback are critical to real time control of the budget. Monitoring the budget is a continuous process managers must complete.

Chapter Summary

- A budget is used to plan and controls optimal use of allocated resources, contains the organizations objectives, and how to obtain the resources needed.

- The types of budgets are: Master Budget, Planned Operating Budget and Financial Budget.

- To meet the organizations goals and objectives, budgets must be coordinated across all departments.

- A flexible operating budget details the budgeted expenses and revenues at different levels of output.

- Zero based budgeting starts with a budget of zero and requires justification for each dollar allocated.

- To implement a budget most effectively, organizations should have top management support, collaborative goal setting, communicating results, flexibility, and follow-up on the process.

- Budget Variance is the difference between the actual cost and the flexible budget.

- For the budgets to be implemented effectively, one needs Top Management support, collaborative goal setting, Communicating results, Flexibility and Follow up and feedback.

Quiz

1. **Which of the following are true about budget plans?**

    a. Budget plans help to utilize the resources efficiently and effectively

    b. Details of the organization's objectives and how to mobilize the resources required are available in a budget plan.

    c. Possible changes to daily operations and staffing are included in a budget plan

    d. All of the above

2. **Which of the following is not correct?**

    a. Coordination of the budget plans of all departments is not important

    b. The master budget is simply the planned operating budget and the finance budget.

    c. The planned operating budget produces a projected income statement.

    d. The financial budget produces a projected balance sheet.

3. **Which of the following is not relevant for the manufacturing cost center budget**

    a. Direct material cost per unit

    b. Direct labor cost per unit

    c. Overhead per unit

    d. Marketing cost per unit

4. Which of the following statements is not correct?

   a. Zero-based budgeting is the simplest form involving lesser paperwork

   b. In zero budgeting, managers start their budgets at zero and justify every dollar placed in the budget

   c. The difference between the actual costs and the flexible budget is called budget variance

   d. In a flexible budget, we can look at the budget in relation to the actual level of output

5. In order to implement budgets and plans most effectively, which of the following are required?

   a. Top management support and collaborative goal setting

   b. Flexibility and follow-up

   c. Discussion of the budget and budget progress

   d. All of the above

| **Answers** | 1 – d | 2 – a | 3 – d | 4 – a | 5 – d |

This page is intentionally left blank

Chapter 7

Problem Solving

Every day, we solve problems both personally and professionally. When you are problem solving, you are finding answers for difficult issues. Often people confuse problem solving and decision making. Problem solving is a method used to solve a specific problem where decision making is a procedure used to during the act of problem solving. Problem solving is analyzing a larger problem at hand while decision making is determining a specific action to take.

Key learning objectives of this chapter include the reader's understanding of the following:

- Basic steps to solve a problem
- Common tools that can be used to define and identify a problem
- Resolving complex problems with the help of different types of tools.

> - Three all-inclusive processes that aid in Problem Solving: Simplex, Appreciative inquiry, and Soft systems methodology.

When solving a problem, you want to go through some basic steps:

- Describe the problem.
- Develop options or alternatives.
- Examine and choose an option.
- Implement the solution.

7.1 Define the Problem

The first step when problem solving is always to describe or state the problem. This piece is critical to finding the right solution the first time. Remember, you are stating the problem and not the symptoms. For example, you have a customer who is very unhappy and has written a letter to your executive team expressing dissatisfaction with a particular widget your company manufactures. The customer indicates he or she has purchased this widget three times and each time it has broken within the first three months of purchase. Your problem is the widget breaks within three months of purchase. The symptom is the customer is dissatisfied.

The other piece of defining the problem is to look at it from an array of perspectives. If you fail to do this, your problem statement can look more like a solution. We may state the problem as, "We must have some kind of guarantee for widget malfunctions." In this case, we aren't getting to the root of the issue which is why the widget is malfunctioning.

Defining the problem can be a challenging process. Below are some tools you can use to assist you in this process:

- **5 Whys –**

    - Assemble a group having knowledge of the issue.
    - Define the issue.
    - Ask the group the first "Why?" – Ask the team why this problem appears to be happening.
    - Ask the group "Why?" four more times. – This step reminds me of an inquisitive 5-year-old who asks
    - "Why?" at the end of every response from their parent. Essentially, you are doing the same thing in this process.
    - Example:
        - Why were the charges entered for Monday lower than projected? Because the doctor saw fewer patients.
        - Why did the doctor see fewer patients? Because a patient left because the doctor was running behind schedule.
        - Why was the doctor running behind schedule? Becaus Mr. Smith's visit took 45 minutes instead of the 15 minutes that was scheduled.
        - Why did Mr. Smith's visit take 45 minutes?

Because Mr. Smith was incorrectly scheduled as a return patient instead of a new patient.

- Why was Mr. Smith scheduled as a return patient? Because we have a new scheduler that started Monday that did not research whether Mr. Smith had been seen by this doctor before.

- **Appreciation** – Similar to the 5 Whys technique, this tool is used to get as much detail as possible out of a fact or statement as possible by asking "So what?"

  - Example: Our staffing is going to be reduced by 25% beginning Aug. 1.

    - So what? So, in order to prepare for this cut, we will have to identify who we will cut from staff.

    - So what? So, if we cut from staff, we will have to figure out how the work of four people will get done with three people.

    - So what? So, we will probably have to take on additional responsibilities from the person who is let go.

    - So what? So, staff may have to work longer hours to complete this work.

    - So what? So, our labor costs may increase due to overtime.

- **Root Cause Analysis –** This technique is one of the more often used to answer questions about why an issue is happening. The goal is to find the origin of the issue using defined steps. These steps are:

    - Define the issue
    - Collect information
    - Detail the possible causes
    - Determine what the root cause(s) is
    - Identify, recommend, and implement solutions

7.2 Understanding Intricacies

Simple problems have simple resolutions and do not require the detailed approach listed above. The more complex the problem, the greater the need for a defined method to find a solution.

There are tools available that can help give you a clearer picture of the issue. The most common tools used are:

- **Affinity diagrams –** This tool collects large amounts of data and sorts them into groups by natural correlation.

Figure 7.1

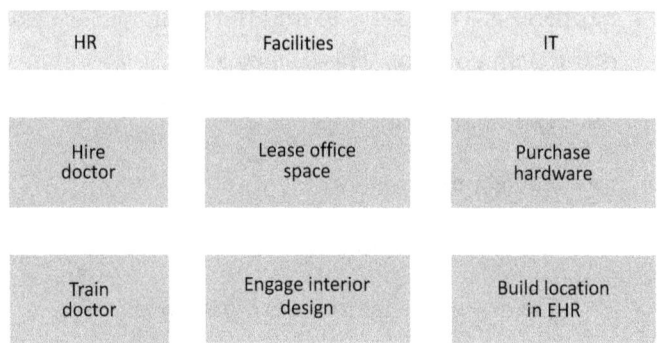

- **Cause and effect diagrams** – Also known as a fishbone or Ishikawa diagram, this tool visualizes categories of possible causes of an issue to aid in detecting the root cause.

Figure 7.2

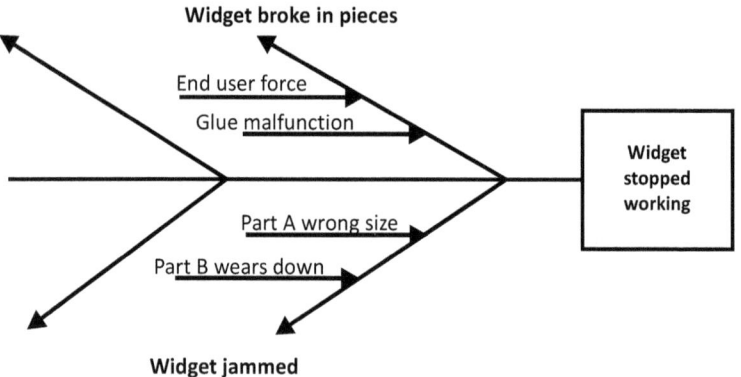

- **Flow charts** – This diagram shows the sequence of activities a person or thing goes through.

Figure 7.3

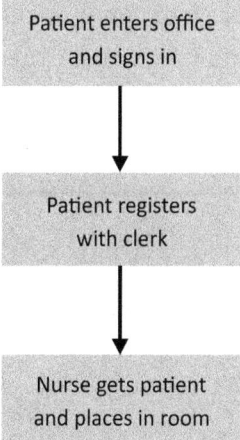

- **Swim lane diagrams** – This diagram is used in conjunction with a flow chart to distinguish between responsibilities of a process.

Figure 7.4

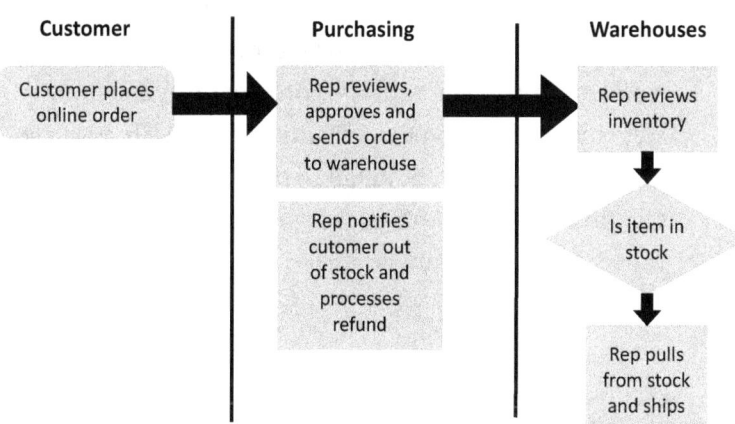

- **System diagrams** – This tool is an excellent way to break down how intricate or complex systems work and how each component of the system affects another.

Figure 7.5

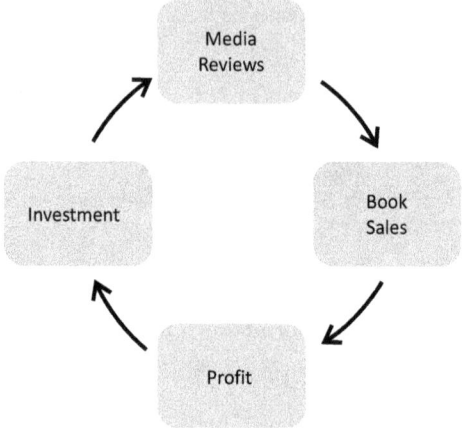

- **Drill down technique** – This tool is used for problems that are so complex they can be broken down into smaller parts to aid in proper problem solving. Simply state the problem on the left side of paper. Then, write down the next level of detail to the right of that problem. Continue to repeat this procedure until you have all the contributing factors detailed out based on what you know.

7.3 Processes to Aid in Problem Solving

Many problems can be solved by using the four-step process at the beginning of this section. However, there are other tools you should have in your problem-solving tool belt. For a more all-inclusive process you can use the following:

- **Simplex** – Simplex is an eight-part process including:

    - **Problem finding** – Ensure you are finding the problem and not just looking at symptoms.

    - **Fact finding** – Find out what the facts say about the problem.

    - **Defining the problem** – Define the specific problem you intend to address.

    - **Idea finding** – Brainstorm possible problem-solving ideas either alone or with groups of people.

    - **Evaluation and selection** – Analyze the ideas generated and determine which one is the best to move forward with.

    - **Planning** – Plan how you intend to implement the idea or solution.

    - **Sell the idea** – Get buy in from stakeholders on the solution.

    - **Action** – Put the plan into place.

- **Appreciative inquiry** – Look at the situation and determine how you can build off the positives. In this method, you ask questions that encourage positive thinking in areas such as:

- **Discover** – Start by asking questions that discover what process works well in an organization.

- **Imagine** – Next, take the information you found from the "discover" step and brainstorm how you can apply that in other areas.

- **Design** – Put together an action plan for implementing the best idea.

- **Deliver** – How will you know if the action plan was successful? Detail out how you will determine what success looks like.

- **Soft Systems Methodology (SSM)** – This methodology is great for problems where there are multiple factors that contribute to the issue and different views to consider. Much has been published about this methodology because it is quite detailed and complex. In its simplest form, the methodology can be described in seven steps:

    - Enter situation considered problematic
    - Express the problem situation
    - Formulate root definitions of relevant systems of purposeful behavior
    - Build conceptual model of human activity systems
    - Compare models with the real world
    - Define changes that are both desirable and feasible

Chapter Summary

- There are four steps to problem solving; describe the problem, develop options or alternatives, examine & choose an option and implement the solution.

- Tools one can use to define the problem : 5 whys (why is the problem occurring), appreciation (so what?), and root cause analysis (define the issue, collect information, detail the possible cause, determine the core cause, detail a solution.

- To form a clearer understanding of the issues at hand, utilize affinity diagrams (natural correlation), cause and effect diagrams (fishbone to detect root cause), flow charts (sequence of activities), swim lane diagrams (distinguish responsibilities), system diagrams (cause and effect within a system), and the drill down technique (solved through smaller problems).

Quiz

1. Which of the following is an incorrect statement on the process of defining a problem?

    a. 5 why strategy involves asking 'why' consecutively upon getting a response

    b. Appreciation strategy involves appreciating each time upon getting a response

    c. Root cause analysis is used to find the origin of the problem

    d. To get as much detail as possible by asking 'So what' after getting a response

2. Which of the following is not a tool for handling complex problems?

    a. Flow charts

    b. Simplex

    c. Drill down technique

    d. Swim lane diagram

3. Which one of the following is also called a Fishbone diagram?

    a. Affinity diagram

    b. Cause and effect diagram

    c. Swim lane diagram

    d. System diagram

4. This tool is used for problems that are complex and can be broken down into smaller parts

   a. System diagram

   b. Swim lane diagram

   c. Drill down technique

   d. Ishikawa diagram

5. One of the all-inclusive processes, which uses 'Discover → Imagine → Design → Deliver' steps is called _____

   a. Simplex process

   b. Appreciative inquiry

   c. Soft systems methodology

   d. None of the above

| **Answers** | 1 – b | 2 – b | 3 – b | 4 – c | 5 – b |

This page is intentionally left blank

Chapter 8

Group Dynamics

Working in an organization, not only as a manager but other roles as well, you will have the opportunity to work with different groups and teams. It is vital that you understand group dynamics, so you can make sure you are utilizing the right approaches when working with them. When people participate in a group, their attitudes and behaviors are influenced by one another as well as the group as a whole. This concept is known as group dynamics. In group dynamics, you focus on how the groups form, how they are structured and what processes they may use in their day-to-day functioning.

Key learning objectives of this chapter include the reader's understanding of the following:

- Stages of group formation namely Forming, Storming, Norming, Performing, and Adjourning

> - Characteristics of different variants of formal and informal groups
> - Factors affecting group behavior
> - Causes of poor group dynamics

A group consists of two or more members who come together for a common purpose or goal. Characteristics of a group are:

- More than one person
- Defined social structure
- Common destiny
- Common purpose or goal
- Interaction between all members
- Interdependence
- Individuals define their role in the group
- Recognition that each person belongs

People typically join groups for various reasons including:

- Affiliation
- Identification
- Emotional support
- Aid
- Common interests
- Common goals
- Physical location

- Mandatory assignment
- Perception of power

8.1 Stages of Group Development

There is a science behind how groups come together and grow as a group. The process is divided into five stages that include:

- Forming
- Storming
- Norming
- Performing
- Adjourning

In the forming stage, members are just convening. They are coming together as a group and looking for the reasons why they are participating in the group. They ask, "What is in it for me?" Some reasons a group may form are for work assignments, status, power, or affiliation. At this time, there is not much emotional investment in the group, so members are apathetic and may engage in busy work.

During storming, emotional investment begins. Members seek out each other according to similarities or familiarities. They begin sharing information about themselves with each other. The group is not a cohesive unit yet. It is common for members to pair off or form their own subgroups. This segmentation can cause conflict amongst group members and controlling the group as a whole becomes an issue.

Norming is where the group members begin to realize they will have to bridge some of the gaps between subgroups if they want to become more accomplished. Members reach out to each other regardless of whether they have anything in common. Their purpose now is to define task performance standards and hold themselves accountable. Group members take responsibility for their part of the work to be accomplished. As a result, the group leader relaxes. Towards the end of this stage a natural hierarchy of leadership is well known, and the group comes together as a whole to achieve its goal. The group has a rapport and camaraderie.

At this point, the group is performing. The members are fully functional and identify as a part of the group. They get involved in activities. The leader is seen more as a part of the group and makes a contribution to the work with the other group members. Team members follow the group norms and rules established in earlier stages. They hold each other accountable for upholding these norms. This activity ensures the group is effective. Goals for the group may change during this stage due to outside information and the group has a "will" to accomplish those goals. The group is now solidifying as a long-term unit either formally or informally.

If the group came together under temporary circumstances, then they go through the last stage of adjourning as the project ends. At this point, the group dissolves and members may be happy about their performance or sad the group is coming to an end.

It is important to note the stages listed above are not always followed sequentially. Groups can also cycle through these stages several times during their life cycle.

8.2 Group Types

Formal

Groups can be either formal or informal. A formal group is convened by an organization to achieve its goals. Formal groups can be classified into either a command, task, or functional group.

A command group has an organizational chart that guides their roles in the group. Typically, the group has a manager or supervisor and the remainder of the group reports to that manager.

A task group includes a collection of people working together to complete a specific activity. This group is also known as a task force and generally has a narrow range of objectives to complete

for a certain period of time. A task force may be charged with developing a new product or service or analyzing a current process for improvements.

A functional group is convened to achieve specific objectives with no specific time frame. These groups are usually longer term and remain a group after the objective is reached. A functional group could be a finance department, patient satisfaction department, or a corporate marketing department.

Informal

An informal group comes together due to common interests or relationships. These groups should not be overlooked because they can have strong positive or negative influences on the organization. Typically, you can sort these informal groups into three categories: interest, friendship, and reference groups.

An interest group consists of people that came together due to a common interest. These groups come together for their own reasons and tend to last longer than other informal groups. They may or may not be related to organizational goals.

A friendship group is created when people get together because they enjoy taking part in the same activities, beliefs, and values. These groups tend to extend their relationship building into after work activities. An example of this group could be a fitness group, a religious group, or a political group.

People evaluate themselves by voluntarily formed reference groups. The purpose of the reference group is for comparison and validation on a social level. Examples of reference groups could be families, friends, or church groups.

8.3 Factors in Group Behavior

There are many factors affecting group behavior. It is important managers understand these factors, so they can help affect positive changes in groups they are working with. The factors are:

- **Group member resources** – What do the individual members of the group bring to the table? This includes knowledge, skill sets, abilities, personal characteristics, etc.

- **Group structure** – Size, roles, norms, and cohesiveness amongst groups are what we look at when we are examining group structure.

- **Group size –**
  - Smaller groups are considered more effective because the group is small enough so each member can be effectively engaged.
  - Larger groups spend more time on how they will function together which decreases their effectiveness.
  - Some experts believe the size of the group can affect the satisfaction of the group members. As the membership increases above 10-12, satisfaction is adversely affected. Cohesion is a main problem for larger groups.

- **Group roles –**
  - Roles in groups are either assigned or emergent. Roles are assigned in formal groups where emergent roles happen organically.
  - As the groups grow, team member comfort levels grow, and they become more assertive. The emergent roles that have developed begin to replace some of the assigned roles. Group roles can then be categorized into work, maintenance, and blocking roles.
  - One group role classification is work role. This role is solely focused on the task at hand and accomplishing goals and objectives assigned to the group. Specific roles include initiator, informer, clarifier, summarizer, and reality tester.

Table 8.1

Initiator	Shows initiative in identifying issues, offering suggested actions and procedures
Informer	Researches facts and provides opinions and guidance
Interpreter	Clarifies ideas, terms, and problems
Summarizer	Summarizes suggestions, promotes decisions, and draws conclusions
Reality Tester	Looks at ideas and tests in terms of real world application

- Maintenance roles help to maintain member participation and engagement in the group. Specific roles include harmonizer, gatekeeper, consensus tester, encourager and compromiser.

Table 8.2

Harmonizer	Acts as a mediator to reduce tensions, reconcile conflict and research opportunities
Gatekeeper	Encourages communications by drawing others to participate, making suggestions, and reiterating open communication channels
Consensus tester	Queries group as a decision emerges and tests possible outcomes
Encourager	Provides encouragement, warmth, friendship, and a welcoming attitude to members
Compromiser	Identifies possible compromises, helps to modify decisions and admits any errors

- Blocking roles disturb the progress of the group. These roles introduce disagreement, resistance, and hidden agendas to the group's activities. Blocking roles do not always produce negative behaviors. Sometimes those behaviors can be positive such as cracking a joke during a tense moment. Specific roles include aggressor, blocker, dominator, comedian, and avoidance behavior

Table 8.3

Aggressor	Antagonizes members by attacking their values and making sarcastic jokes in a derogatory manner
Blocker	Characterized as stubborn and resistant and will disagree with group members frequently
Dominator	With a goal of controlling discussion, this role is known for patronizing group members
Comedian	Also known as the class clown, this role wants attention at the expense of the group's objectives
Avoidance Behavior	Not interested in maintaining focus on the groups object, so this role will change the subject and avoid commitment.

- Group cohesiveness –
    - Described as how the group members get along, how well they bond or feel unity, and what their level of desire is to be a part of the group.
    - If maintaining membership in the group is difficult to achieve, then cohesiveness will be an ongoing issue. Steady membership allows for a unity to grow amongst the members.

- If in a competition setting, groups are more likely to create cohesiveness amongst members.

- Cohesiveness is also increased in smaller groups who spend more time together.

- Cohesiveness in groups has both positive and negative effects. On one hand, employee satisfaction and production are higher when turnover and absenteeism are reduced. On the other hand, a very cohesive group not affiliated with organizational objectives can be very damaging to organizational performance.

- As group cohesiveness increases, the risk of groupthink increases as well. Groupthink occurs when group members pressure one another to come to an agreement during decision making. Groupthink can result in bad judgement, reduced reality testing, and unrealistic expectations.

- Groups typically outperform individuals and benefit from motivational aspects as well. Decision making and problem-solving participation is higher in groups which generate empowerment and productivity. The bulk of work completed in organizations is completed by groups; therefore, the effectiveness of the organization is determined by the effectiveness of the group.

- **Group processes –**
  - Decision making can be better in a group because the group benefits from the varied knowledge of the members.
  - The downside to group decision making is it can be a lengthy process, group members can pressure one another to change their decision, and there is little accountability in a group decision.

8.4 Causes of Poor Group Dynamics

If your group is experiencing poor group dynamics, the following list shows some common issues to look for and tackle in these circumstances.

- **Ineffective leadership** – Groups with ineffective leaders often see a dominant member try to lead the group. This results in inefficiencies such as lack of direction, focus on incorrect priorities, and fighting amongst members.

- **Excessive agreeance to leadership** – People fail to express their opinions and prefer to agree with authority.

- **Blocking** – Group members interrupt the flow of information within the group. This is done through roles such as:
  - **The aggressor** – Very outspoken to the point of inappropriateness, this person is usually at the center of disagreements.

- **The negator** – This person is known for shooting down others' ideas and suggestions.

- **The withdrawer** – The withdrawer is the person in the group who doesn't participate.

- **The recognition seeker** – This person is known to dominate the discussion and boasts of their accomplishments.

- **The joker** – This person can be identified as the class clown. Always joking, this person uses humor in every situation including inappropriate ones.

- **Groupthink** – A great example of this would be in a jury. In an effort to reach consensus instead of reaching the right decision, they are prevented from really exploring all options.

- **Free riding** – This person rides the group's coattails and lets other members do the bulk of the work. This person may work hard individually but limits the work contributed to the group.

- **Evaluation apprehension** – Group members hold back their opinions due to a fear of being judged too harshly by other group members.

Chapter Summary

- A group consists of two or more members who come together for a common purpose or goal.

- The five stages of group development are forming, storming, norming, performing, and adjourning.

- The forming stages consist of members convening as a group.

- The storming stage involves members becoming emotionally invested and potentially causes segmentation with the group.

- The norming stage is when members realize the gap between subgroups and work to bridge the gaps.

- The performing stage requires one, fully functional group where members hold each other accountable for upholding the norms and begin working to one goal.

- The adjourning stage happens when a group is formed under temporary circumstances. The group will dissolve, and the project will come to a close.

- Informal groups consist of three categories: interest, friendship, and reference groups.

- An interest group consists of members with a common interest.

- A friendship group involves members who enjoy the same activities, beliefs, and values

- A reference group is formed for comparison and validation on a social level.

- The two main factors of group behavior are member resources and group structure. Group member resources are the traits specific to each member and utilized during the project, while the group structure revolves around size, roles and norms.

- There are five types of roles in a group: aggressor, blocker, dominator, comedian, and avoidance behavior.

- Poor group dynamics are typically due to ineffective leadership, excessive agreeance to leadership, blocking, groupthink, free riding, and evaluation apprehension.

Quiz

1. Which of the following pair does not represent the characteristics of a Group?

    a. More than one person and defined social structure

    b. Common destiny and common purpose or goal

    c. Aloofness among members and independence

    d. Role definition by individuals and recognition that each member belongs

2. Which of the following statements is wrong?

    a. During the Storming stage, emotional investment begins

    b. Norming is the stage when group members realize bridging gaps in sub-group is required

    c. At the Performing stage, members are fully functional and identify as a part of the group

    d. The stages of group development strictly occur in the order of 'Storming → Forming → Norming → Performing

3. Which of the following is a wrong statement about a formal group?

    a. Command group has an organizational chart that guides the roles of the group members.

    b. A task group includes a collection of people working to complete a specific activity

c. A functional group is convened to achieve specific objectives without any time frame.

d. A reference group is also a formal group.

4. Which of the following is an incorrect statement about an informal group?

    a. Informal groups come together due to common interests or relationships

    b. There are three categories of informal groups namely interest, friendship, and reference groups.

    c. These groups can be overlooked in an organization as they do not have much influence

    d. People evaluate themselves by voluntarily formed reference groups

5. Which of the following statements best describes a group role?

    a. As groups grow, team member comfort levels also grow

    b. Roles in groups are either assigned or emergent

    c. Group roles are classified into work, maintenance, and block roles

    d. All of the above

| Answers | 1 – c | 2 – d | 3 – d | 4 – c | 5 – d |

Chapter 9

Converting a Group to a Successful Team

Not all groups would be considered a team. It is important to understand where your group currently stands so you can understand what the next steps would be to ensure you have a successful team.

> Key learning objectives of this chapter include the reader's understanding of the following:

- Difference between a group and a team
- The nature and uses of problem-solving teams, self-managed teams, cross-functional teams, virtual teams, institutional teams, and operational teams.
- Approaches to improving team dynamics

9.1 Group vs. Team

The text below gives you a quick reference to determine if you have a group or a team.

Group

- Work is not engaged in collectively even though a joint effort is required
- No positive collaboration to generate new ideas or suggestions
- Performance of the group is not improved with each members contribution
- Responding to changing environments is a challenge.

Team

- Team members work together and individually with team accountability as well as individual accountability
- Team members bounce ideas off one another generating new ideas and positive collaboration. The group uses its collective knowledge to address a problem. The members work to tackle larger tasks are too large for any one individual to address
- Outcomes are better with a team and does not require an increase in their individual contributions

- Dynamic environments are not as challenging because teams are typically agile and more responsive.

To convert a group to a team, team building is used. Team building brings members together and encourages them to share with one another in understanding each other's perceptions and views. Activities such as rope courses, getting-to-know-you games, team outings, etc. are commonly used team building activities.

The following are some tips to promote team building:

- Define expectations at the onset. Managers are responsible for telling the team members the expectations of performance and the reason for the team to come together. The organization leadership should clearly understand what is required for the team to be successful, so it can support the team with resources such as personnel and money.

- Team members must be committed to the successful achievement of the team's goals and objectives. When team members feel their contributions are valuable to their organization and their own careers, they will likely demonstrate the commitment needed.

- Team members should have the right skillset to accomplish the task at hand.

- Team members should be accountable for their progress and success. They should also be empowered to accomplish goals and objectives.

- Team members should actively collaborate with one another. Collaboration is more likely to occur if team members understand each of their roles and responsibilities.

- Communication amongst team members and from leadership to team members should happen timely and often. The team should be aware of what they are to accomplish as well as how they are performing to expectations.

- Forge an environment of creativity. Always encourage team members to think outside of the box, create unique solutions and present new ideas.

Figure 9.1

There are six types of teams to be aware of:

- **Problem-solving teams** – The sole purpose of these teams is to resolve an identified problem or problems.

- **Self-managed teams** – These teams are self-directed with no formal manager. Team members work together to put together a plan of their day-to-day activities and responsibilities.

- **Cross-functional teams** – Teams consisting of various experts from different areas working towards a common objective.

- **Virtual teams** – Geographically spread out teams working together from different locations by using technology such as email, video conferencing, phone, and instant messaging.

- **Institutional teams** – Teams pertaining to the entirety of an organization or corporation, with membership in the hundreds.

- **Operational teams** – Membership is smaller, coming in contact daily, and each member contributes to achieve the objective.

9.2 Approaches to Improving Team Dynamics

At some point in your career, you may be asked to lead a group of people to achieve a task or goal. To be successful in achieving that goal for the organization, you may be challenged with improving the team dynamics. Below are some approaches to accomplishing this task.

- **Be familiar with your team** – Understand where in the group process your team is situated. Is it forming, storming, norming, performing, or adjourning? When you know this, you can be proactive about problems that may come up and how you will address them. Understanding the different roles in a group helps you identify the positive and negative forces in the group so you can preemptively solve future issues.

- **Address problems promptly** – Problems that arise should be addressed quickly because the longer they continue, the harder it will be to resolve them. Frequently provide feedback to team members so they are aware of how their actions affect the group. Encourage team members to promote behavior helpful to the group.

- **Ensure roles and responsibilities are clearly defined** – When team members do not understand their roles in the group, work becomes inefficient and ineffective. Team members spend time trying to figure out how they fit in the group instead of collaborating with others to accomplish the goal. One way to combat this is with a team charter. Team charters clearly define the mission and objectives of the team, what each person's role is, and what his or her responsibilities are.

- **Remove barriers to success** – Start with team building exercises early on so each member gets to know one another. Team building exercises may need to be done several times throughout the life of the group due to new team members or conflicts that arise. Encourage team members to open up to one another so real cohesiveness can develop and clear alignment of goals and objectives can be established.

- **Communicate, communicate, communicate** – Ensure you have a communication plan that includes all forms of communication, so you can reach each of the team members. Encourage open communication and communicate often.

- **Pay Attention** – Stay alert for warning signs your group dynamics are declining. One telltale sign to look for is unanimous decisions. If your group is frequently coming to unanimous decisions, some group members may be being bullied or groupthink is occurring.

Chapter Summary

♦ A group does not collectively engage in the work, lacks collaborations for new ideas or suggestions, performance is not based on member contribution, and responding to changing environments is challenging.

♦ A team works together, observes accountability, new ideas are generated through positive collaborations to address a problem, outcome requires fewer individual contributions, and dynamic environments are not a challenge.

♦ A group is converted into a team through team building. The six types of teams are problem solving, self-managed, cross-functional, virtual, institutional, and operational.

♦ To improve team dynamics, be familiar with your team, address problems promptly, ensure roles and responsibilities are clearly defined, remove barriers to success, communicate and pay attention to the group's functionality.

Quiz

1. Which of the following statements best describes the characteristics of a group

   a. Performance is not improved with each member's contribution

   b. Responding to changing environments is a challenge

   c. No positive collaboration to generate new ideas or suggestions

   d. All of the above

2. Which of the following statements is not applicable to the characteristics of a team?

   a. Team members work to tackle larger tasks that are too large for any individual to address

   b. Outcomes are better with team contribution as a whole

   c. Team members need not work individually as there is no individual accountability

   d. A dynamic environment does not pose a challenge as teams are typically agile and responsive

3. Which of the following is essentially expected from management for team building

   a. Commitment

   b. The right skill set

   c. Accountability

   d. Defining expectations at the onset

4. Which of the following statements best describes the tips for team building

    a. Collaboration with one another within the team

    b. Communication amongst team members

    c. Creativity of team members

    d. All of the above

5. 'Membership is smaller, coming in contact on a daily basis with each member contributing to achieve objectives'– is the characteristic of which of the following teams?

    a. Operational teams

    b. Institutional teams

    c. Virtual teams

    d. Cross-functional teams

| **Answers** | 1 – d | 2 – c | 3 – d | 4 – d | 5 – a |

Chapter **10**

Conflict Resolution

Conflict happens in the workplace due to different personalities, values, goals, and objectives. Conflict appears because different people have different needs. Dictionary.com defines conflict as a serious disagreement or argument. With this definition, you may think that all conflict is negative. Although there are definitely conflicts that cause animosity and result in broken relationships, some conflict can be positive. Conflict can be positive when hidden issues are brought to light and you are increasing understanding of an issue. Sometimes just going through the conflict and resolving it improves the cohesion of a team. Conflict can also help people see views and perspectives they would not have normally seen if they had relied on their own self-knowledge.

As a manager, you have an opportunity to affect whether conflict is positive or negative. If conflict festers with no resolution, it will most likely have negative effects. Therefore, it is critical that you immediately address the conflict with a proven approach to help it become a positive exercise for the team or individuals involved.

> Key learning objectives of this chapter include the reader's understanding of the following:
>
> - Types of conflicts
> - Healthy and unhealthy conflict resolution actions
> - Conflict management strategies

10.1 Types of Conflict

Conflict can occur among groups, individuals, internally, etc. The following list details the different types of conflicts:

- **Interpersonal conflict** – involves conflict between two people. This is a common conflict that arises due to differing personalities. Sometimes calling in a third person to mediate is a helpful solution.

- **Intrapersonal conflict** – is when a person is having a conflict within himself, also known as an inner conflict. Often, speaking to others about one's concerns helps to release the anxiety felt. This type of conflict often leads to personal growth and empowerment.

- **Intragroup conflict** – is conflict that happens amongst team members. Usually, interpersonal conflicts lead to intragroup conflicts. Sometimes this conflict can be helpful for coming to a joint decision. Other times, exacerbated intragroup conflict negatively affects the synergy of the group. In this case, the group leader would need to step in and guide the team to a resolution.

- **Intergroup conflict** – happens when different teams in the organization disagree. Often, this conflict is due to differing goals and objectives for each team. Competition and rivalry can also be factors that affect intergroup conflict.

10.2 Healthy vs. Unhealthy Conflict Management

People handle conflict in different ways according to their experiences, values, training, and personality. It is important to understand actions that are healthy and unhealthy in coming to resolution. The text below helps to identify this.

Healthy Conflict Resolution Actions

- Empathizing with another's viewpoint
- Reacting calmly, respectfully, and not defensively
- Willingness to get past the conflict with a forgive and forget attitude
- Attempting to compromise without retribution
- Believing that facing conflict directly is the best approach

Unhealthy Conflict Resolution Actions

- Not caring about the other person's interests or point of view
- Reacting with anger, upset, explosiveness and resentfulness
- Unwilling to forgive, threatening to withdraw love with rejection and isolation of the other party
- Inability to put yourself in another's shoes
- Being afraid of conflict and therefore avoiding it altogether

10.3 Conflict Management Strategies

There are several different strategies used to manage conflict. It is helpful to understand these strategies as you work to resolve conflict with other people and teams. Knowing these strategies as well as being able to utilize them will help you be a more effective mediator in conflict.

Accommodating

This occurs when a person gives in to the demands of the other person in the conflict. This approach is performed in an effort to keep the peace. For those who do not like conflict, it may seem like a quick and easy resolution to the issue. However, there may be a need to come up with a more creative solution. This approach is best used when the accommodating person is wrong and uses this as a way to reconcile the issue.

Avoiding

Avoiding is when you completely remove yourself from the conflict. Typically, those who utilize this method think the possible negative outcomes are worse than the positive outcomes. They decide to ignore the problem in the hopes the problem will go away or resolve itself. When this approach is used, the other party may interpret your avoidance as neglecting the issue. Although it may be useful in some cases the issue should be confronted more often than not.

Collaboration

Collaboration is the action of really understanding each party's side of the issue in an effort to arrive at a satisfactory resolution for everyone involved. This approach helps each party avoid giving up something in return for a resolution. Each party's interest is preserved.

Competing

Competing is characterized by aggressive behaviors used by a person to assert pressure on other parties to come into agreement. This approach asks the other party to give up their goals and interests and adopt the other person's viewpoint. There may be a situation where this approach is appropriate, but it is no longer useful if the aggressor becomes unreasonable.

Compromising

Compromising looks for a resolution that meets each parties' needs. It is essentially a mutual give-and-take where each party invests an equal amount in the resolution. A downside to this strategy is that typically all of the parties' interests are not met. Also, this technique can fail to find more creative solutions when the problem is easily resolved with a compromise.

Interest Based Relational Approach (IBR)

This approach says it is the manager's responsibility to ensure team members are respected and heard as well as to resolve the conflict. Team members want their viewpoints to be understood and their differences appreciated. Basically, the manager is the referee in the game of conflict, ensuring that everyone acts in an adult manner and that a consensus is achieved.

In order for the IBR approach to be the most effective, several skills must be practiced. Listening actively and empathetically is vitally important to each person feeling understood and appreciated. Understanding body language and having emotional intelligence will allow you to see the hidden issues that need to be brought to light and addressed. Also, understanding how to manage anger with different techniques will allow you to ensure everyone acts civilly.

Managers should be aware of the following steps:

- Relationships are most important. Preserving the relationships should be on the forefront during the entire conflict resolution process.

- Set ground rules for conflict discussion. Examples of rules may be:
    - Keep your emotions in check.
    - Use words accurately portraying your feelings instead of actions.
    - Don't beat around the bush. Be specific about your concern.
    - Specify the issue to work on and do not move outside of that topic.
    - Don't play dirty. Attacking someone personally is not appropriate.
    - Instead of accusing, describe how the actions of another made you feel.
    - Avoid generalizations.
    - Be honest and do not exaggerate.
    - Do not store up grievances and then unpack all of them on the other person.
    - Keep the conversation going. Don't withdraw or clam up. The only way to a resolution is continued communication.
- Try to separate the problem from the people. Clearly defining the problem and understanding the person is not necessarily the problem is key to moving forward. For example, I may say that the bank teller Sue is being spiteful and won't let me cash a check when the actual problem is my account at the bank is closed and it is the bank's policy not to let me cash the check if I do not have an open account.

- Careful listening is key. Listen for key things in the dialogue to tell you why each person is holding tightly to their position.

- Listen more, talk less. The old adage is true: you have two ears and only one mouth, so you can do twice as much listening as talking.

- State the facts. Agreeing on the facts could sway someone's decision.

- Work together to explore other options. There may be another option besides the two you are in conflict about. Be open to that idea.

Negotiation

Another approach to resolving conflict is simple negotiation. When using negotiation, the goals are to devise a solution that is agreed upon by all parties, to expedite the solution, and to advance the relationship rather than hurt it. Below are seven steps to guide you in utilizing negotiation successfully to resolve conflict.

- Comprehend the conflict
- Talk to the opposition
- Brainstorm possible solutions
- Decide which solution is best for both parties
- Involve an outside party as a mediator
- Look at all options and alternatives
- Use coping skills to address stressful situations and pressure tactics.

Figure 10.1

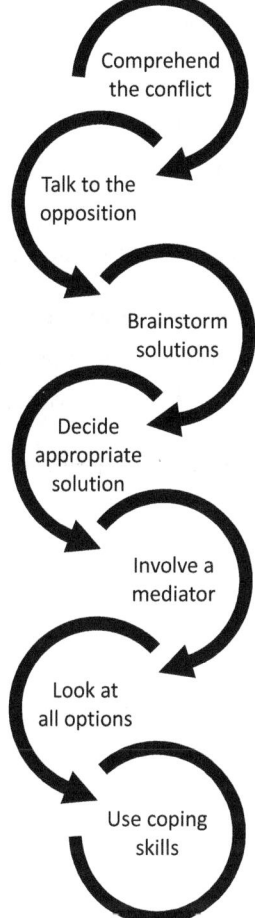

Chapter Summary

- Conflict appears because different people have different needs.

- The four types of conflict are 1) interpersonal (between two people), 2) intrapersonal (inner conflict within oneself), 3) intragroup (between team members), and 4) intergroup (different teams with an organization).

- People should handle conflict in a healthy manner by facing the issue, be willing to get past the issue, attempt to compromise, and empathize with others.

Quiz

1. Competition and rivalry can also cause _____ conflict

   a. Intra group

   b. Intra personal

   c. Interpersonal

   d. Intergroup

2. Which of the following can be termed as healthy conflict resolution action(s)

   a. Resentfulness

   b. Forgive and forget attitude and compromise without retribution

   c. Avoiding the conflict altogether

   d. Options b and c

3. What is the approach to keep the peace by giving into the demands of another person in a conflicting situation called?

   a. Healthy conflict resolution

   b. Unhealthy conflict resolution

   c. Accommodating strategy

   d. Avoiding strategy

4. Each party's interest is preserved in which conflict-handling strategy?

   a. Compromising

   b. Avoiding

   c. Collaboration

   d. Accommodating

5. Which of the following is not true about the interest-based relational approach?

   a. It is the responsibility of the manager to ensure team members are respected and heard when there is a conflict

   b. Listening actively and empathetically is vitally important to each person

   c. This technique may fail to find more creative solutions when the problem is easily resolved.

   d. Understanding body language and having emotional intelligence helps to look at the hidden issues

| **Answers** | 1 – d | 2 – b | 3 – c | 4 – c | 5 – c |

Chapter 11

Communication

Effective communication skills are vitally important in every industry and workplace. Every day you communicate with colleagues, executives, customers, leadership, and team members. It's even more critical today when everything is digitalized and communicated through technology.

Key learning objectives of this chapter include the reader's understanding of the following:

- Communication process and types of communication
- Barriers to effective communication
- Managerial Communication
- Goals and types of listening

First, communication happens in two directions – downward and upward. Downward communication is when a manager communicates to employees. Upward communication occurs when the employees communicate to managers Or when managers communicate upward to other managers.

Figure 11.1

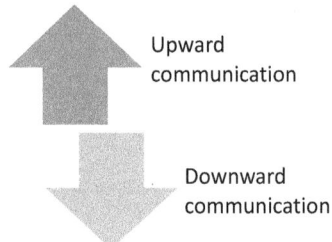

11.1 Communication Process

What happens during communication? In its simplest form, a sender sends a message through a channel of communication to a receiver or receivers. The sender is responsible for putting the message into a format easily understandable by the receiver. The receiver deciphers the message, so they can understand the meaning and importance. Understanding the communication allows you to minimize misunderstandings and overcome barriers at any stage of the process.

Figure 11.2

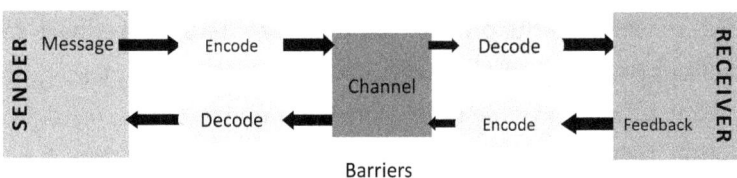

The way you choose to communicate is known as the channel. Examples of a channel may be social media, text, phone call, face to face, email, radio, television, written documents, reports, etc. Choosing the correct channel of communication is critical to an effective message. For example, if you need to get a message out to a large group of people about a change in a policy, utilizing a phone tree (where one person calls another with the info) would not be appropriate because information could become misconstrued during the relay.

Messages must be put into a format that can be communicated with the channel chosen for that particular message. Thoughts will need to be translated into sentences for messages sent through emails and reports. For a brief announcement or commercial, the message would need to be abbreviated. As you are thinking about what form you will use for your message, consider the audience. If this is a discussion on financial performance for the past three years, a visual report such as a graph may be more effective for your financial team to see trends rather than a few written paragraphs.

When the receiver gets the message, they interpret what is being communicated. Interpretation of the message can be affected by context, emotions, the external environment, personal bias, etc. The sender should try to anticipate how the message can be interpreted to aid in avoiding any misunderstandings.

The last stage of the process is the receiver returns feedback to the sender based on what they have decoded from the message. The receiver may provide both verbal and nonverbal indicators as to how they interpreted the message. At this time, the sender should examine the feedback closely to ensure that the message sent was interpreted correctly.

11.2 Communication Types

In order to fully understand all aspects of communication, let's first take a look at the different types of communication:

- Verbal
- Written modes
- Body language
- Facial expressions
- Gestures

The most common form of communication is verbal communication. In verbal communications, instructions, information, and feedback are communicated orally with words. When verbally communicating, it is important to pay attention to your word choices to ensure you are clearly understood. You also want to be conscious of your pitch, tone, and volume to confirm you are conveying your message as intended. For example, if you are presenting on a topic as an expert, you want to make sure your tone is assertive to convey confidence. Examples of verbal communications are presentations, meetings, and classes. This type of communication can happen on the phone, face to face, or through video conferencing.

The most commonly used form of written communication is email. The most effective use of this mode of communication is utilizing it as a follow-up to verbal communication. For example, if you hold a meeting, send the participants an email afterwards outlining what was discussed and the action items. Emails are best utilized when they are short and to the point. Pay attention to spelling and grammar in your emails as well as tone. Even though you have typed the words exactly as you have intended, the recipient could read it with another tone and the message becomes something else. As with all documentation, you want to make sure it appears professional, so avoid using all caps, flashy icons or images. Keeping it simple is most professional.

Body language, facial expressions, and gestures are all considered forms of nonverbal communication. How you position your body when you are delivering a message is vitally important to conveying an effective message. People use all five senses when interacting. The bulk of the information is taken in through sight, then through hearing, followed by smell, touch, and taste. If you are trying to congratulate a colleague on a promotion but your body language reads that you aren't really happy for that person, your congratulations will be perceived as insincere. A smile or pleasant look on your face can be perceived by others as welcoming and can encourage them to communicate more often with you. Also, being careful to limit your hand movements while communicating can help reduce the risk of conveying the wrong message. Most importantly, direct eye contact is key if you want the message to be most effective and have the greatest impact.

11.3 Barriers to Effective Communication

Communication is the most vital thing you will do in your career regardless of whether or not you are a manager. Understanding communication and its barriers will help you determine the best ways to navigate through meetings, negotiations and other critical conversations.

- **Language and cultural barriers**
    - The use of jargon, slang, or abbreviations. There are abbreviations for everything in today's world but not everyone is familiar with what they mean. Avoid using them to ensure that your message is clear.
    - Differences in languages and accents
    - Differences in culture
- **Psychological barriers**
    - Emotional barriers or off-limits topics. Expressing your emotions in the workplace is not a strong skill everyone possesses so they will find providing feedback about emotions challenging. Communication involving sensitive topics such as politics or religion will also be challenged as most people are uncomfortable discussing this outside of their close friend group.
    - Personal prejudices or stereotypes can distort the meaning of messages.

- **Physiological barriers**
  - Hearing and speech disabilities

- **Physical barriers**
  - With the bulk of messages being sent through channels that are not face to face, an inability to see nonverbal communication cues is a definite barrier.

- **Systematic barriers**
  - Bias and politics in the workplace are major barriers to effective communication. If employees have preconceived notions about a particular action the organization is taking, they will not hear the message as intended.

- **Attitudinal barriers**
  - Some receivers may not be interested in the message being sent, or they may find the message irrelevant to them. As a result, they do not pay attention, or they become distracted by other more important things.
  - Some receivers may perceive the message differently than it was intended or feel that their perspective or values conflict with the message. If their initial reaction is negative, they will be resistant to understanding your intentions.

11.4 Managerial Communication

How is communication in management different? Why would you say it is even more important for the manager to be an effective communicator than an employee? Communication is at the core of every effective organization. Information, strategies, goals, and objectives are typically communicated through management from the top down. When the manager receives this information to disseminate, he is charged with playing the following roles:

- **Knowledge sharer** – Sharing with his team what you know.

- **Task master** – Communicating with team members to ensure deadlines are met and tasks are completed so organizational goals can be met.

- **Employee liaison** – Creating a level of transparency between teams and their managers.

- **Motivator** – Encouraging team members and creating a level of enthusiasm for reaching the goal. Communicating how their work contributes to the overall organizational goals.

- **Crisis management** – Continuous communication allows managers to address issues quickly and proactively address risks.

- **Stress reliever** – Creating conversation is not just about work. Personal conversations bring lightness and fun to the environment.

Since managers must play all these roles, they must master

effective communications. The following are some essential skills that managers should have in their communication tool belt:

- What is the context? When you are talking to a team member, be sure to answer these questions from their point of view, "what is in it for me?" and "why do I care?" The most critical part of the context to set is the relationship between what the employee is doing and his contributions to the organization's strategic goals and objectives. Show them the big picture.

- If a message is important, don't stop at one communication. Researchers have determined we must hear a message many times in many ways before we fully comprehend it. Know your audience and how they like to receive messages. Don't assume everyone likes the same method of communication.

- Encourage dialogue and check with the recipient to ensure he understands what you meant. Paraphrase what they say back to you to make sure you are on the same page. Ask questions like "what risks do you see with this?" or "what are some advantages of this?"

- Listen, listen, and listen some more. Practice active listening which will be discussed in a later section.

- Utilize calls to action. As you are creating your message and delivering your communication, be sure you are clear in what you are asking the recipient to do with the information. Do you want them to take action? Do you want them to simply listen and be informed?

11.5 General Listening

Merriam-Webster.com defines the word listen as "to hear something with thoughtful attention: give consideration." In your everyday interactions of listening to people talk, would you say you are hearing them with thoughtful attention? Most people would probably say no. With so many distractions in today's world, it is difficult to stay focused on one thing. As a result, listening has become an acquired skill. Arguably, listening is the most important skill one can have.

In general, there are two main categories of listening:

- Discriminative

- Comprehensive

Discriminative listening is the earliest form of listening we develop. Some say we may be developing this skill in the womb. In this type of listening, our goal is to discern different types of sounds but not look for any meaning in them. As you grow older, this skill becomes sharper and you can use it to decipher the difference between voice tones and volumes. It helps you gather insight to nonverbal cues that tell you if the speaker's voice indicates a particular emotion. When you combine this type of listening with your visual sense, you can really begin to determine what body language means. For example, as I am listening to someone talk, their voice sounds weepy and almost as though they are choking back tears. If I was unable to see the person, I would not be able to see the smile on the person's face indicating tears of joy and not tears of sadness.

When we are concentrating on understanding and interpreting the message being communicated, we are practicing comprehensive listening. Comprehensive listening is developed as the person's knowledge of vocabulary and language skills grow. One complicating factor to developing comprehensive listening is influenced by personal biases and points of view. Therefore, you could be speaking to a group of people, tell them all the exact same thing, but they each comprehend totally different messages individually.

If we examine listening a bit closer, we can categorize it into three types of interpersonal communication: informational listening, critical listening, and therapeutic or empathetic listening. These types define the goal of the listening taking place. It is possible to have more than one goal of listening at one point in time.

Goals of Listening

Informational listening happens when you are listening with the goal of learning something. It is very common and happens every day. Children practice informational listening at school, and parents practice it at work. When your friend is showing you the latest dance craze, you are practicing informational listening. This type of listening is said to be less active, meaning we are simply listening to the message to take it in. We are not analyzing or questioning it.

If our goal is to scrutinize the information being delivered, we are engaged in critical listening. As we listen to the message being delivered to us, we are criticizing it and evaluating its validity. Criticize is often used as a negative word to indicate look for flaws or issues but in actuality, it is really just asking more questions about what the speaker is saying to you. "What is the point he or she is trying to make?" or "What does this mean to me?" are examples of questions you may ask while critically listening. It is important while practicing this type of listening to be unbiased and open minded.

Therapeutic or empathic listening is just as it sounds. It is listening for emotion or feelings from the speaker. The listener empathizes and tries to understand the feelings being conveyed attempting to see things through the speaker's eyes. This type of listening is commonly practiced by counselors, therapists, psychologists, etc. An important part of empathic listening is to be nonjudgmental, not offer guidance, and encourage others to continue speaking about their feelings and elaborate more.

Other Types of Listening

Additional types of listening are less commonly used but are helpful to be aware of. Appreciative listening is simply listening for your own enjoyment. Examples are listening to a favorite song or guiding meditation. Rapport listening happens when we are trying to build a relationship with the speaker. The listener is attempting to build trust and persuade the speaker to like him or her. It is commonly used by sales teams to encourage prospective customers to purchase what they are selling. Selective listening is a negative type of listening where you choose what you want to hear both consciously and unconsciously. Typically, this listening occurs when the listener comes into the conversation with a personal bias or preconceived notion.

11.6 Active Listening

Active listening is putting your full focus and concentration on what is being said by a speaker. Although the word listening implies using only one sense-hearing. However, to truly actively listen, you must use all the senses. Actively listening also involves appearing to the speaker you are actually listening using verbal and nonverbal cues. These cues can include eye contact, nodding your head, smiling, and verbal affirmations such as "yes" and "I see". Providing feedback encourages the speaker to continue and feel more at ease.

Below is a list of nonverbal cues that indicate to the speaker you are actively listening:

- Smiling can be used as a way of agreeing or showing empathy as well as understanding.

- Eye contact can demonstrate you are fully focused on what the speaker is saying. It is important to gauge how much eye contact is used since it can be intimidating to some people.

- Posture, like leaning forward, shows the speaker you are interested in what they are saying and essentially asking them to tell you more. Head tilts and other body postures can also show interest.

- Mirroring occurs when the listener automatically reflects the expressions of the speaker. Used appropriately, mirroring can indicate empathy and sympathy to the speaker. If you are consciously trying to mimic facial expressions, this can show you are not paying attention or possibly disrespect. Take care in how this is used.

- Distractions are avoided by active listeners. Active listeners avoid doodling, playing with their hair, looking out the window or at clock, etc.

Below is a list of verbal cues to let the speaker know you are actively listening:

- Positive reinforcement is often used to encourage the speaker to continue. This cue should be used carefully, so as not to put unnecessary emphasis on a particular part of the conversation or cause a distraction.

- Remembering information from previous conversations and appropriately applying them to the current message can demonstrate you understand what is being conveyed.

- Questioning the speaker about relevant details can help clarify the message and demonstrate to the speaker you really seek to understand what they are saying.

- Reflecting information back to the speaker, or repeating or paraphrasing, is a powerful way of showing the speaker you heard what they said, and you understand.

- Clarifying delivered information assures the speaker that you want to make sure the correct message is received.

- Summarizing or repeating back what has been discussed in your own words, gathers the main points of the message together and allows both the speaker and listener to ensure they are on the same page.

Imagine that you are a new manager and you are preparing for a discussion with an employee on a critical matter. You have just read the information above. Now what do you do? Use the principles of active listening listed below as your guide.

- No talking. Put all of your focus on listening to the person speaking. Just listen.

- Get ready to listen. Often times in a crucial conversation, we spend time rolling distracting thoughts around in our heads or planning what we will say next. Relax, clear your mind and be ready to give the speaker your full attention.

- Let the speaker know he or she is safe speaking with you. Remember the nonverbal cues to show understanding and support. Use verbal cues for encouragement. Use eye contact as appropriate for the individual.

- Eliminate distractions. If you are prone to looking out the window at a great view, sit with your back to the window. Remove papers and items from the desk that may tempt you. Turn your phone off so you have no unnecessary distractions.

- Put yourself in the other person's shoes. Show empathy and use an open mind while listening. Try to put any bias or preconceived notions out of your mind.

- A moment without speech is acceptable. Moments of silence are often interpreted as awkward and people are tempted to fill those blanks with conversation. Be patient with the speaker and allow him/her to find the right words to say in their own time.

- Approach the discussion with impartiality. Try to put aside any personal prejudices you may have with the speaker such as how they speak or their mannerisms. Focus on what is being conveyed.

- Volume and tone tell a lot about the message. Pay attention to both items so you can be sure to get the key points that are being emphasized.

- Try to pull together the whole picture and not just fragments. There is usually a larger picture involved in the story that will help your understanding. Take the fragments of information you have and piece them into the larger picture for a better view and understanding.

- Non-verbal communication says everything. Watch for those non-verbal cues to help you decipher if there is an underlying issue that needs to be addressed. When you see those cues, ask the speaker for more clarification on the topic being discussed.

11.7 Tips to Remember about Communication

A lot of information has been presented as a part of this communication section. We have discussed communication processes, types, barriers, managerial communications and active listening. With all this information, it is easy to get lost in the minutiae. As we close this section, let's take a step back to remember the following key things about managerial communication.

- Managers don't sequester themselves in an office. They communicate through interacting with their employees on a regular basis.

- Morning meetings can be advantageous because they can help your team plan their day based on what you are communicating.

- Managers must always be working to improve their listening skills.

- When working in isolation, no communication happens. Working in a team fosters communication amongst each other and with leaders. Utilize this communication channel for messaging.

- Writing an effective email is an important skill for any manager. Ensure that you and your team members have all received proper training to help your emails be the most effective they can be.

- Stop, think, and then speak. Purposefully choose your words when communicating messages to your team members. Be very deliberate in what you say to convey the most accurate message.

- Always follow up for understanding for any message being sent especially with key messages and messages requiring action.

- Deliver team messages to the entire team at one time in a place that has no distractions.

Chapter Summary

- Communication happens in two directions. Downward communication involves a manager communicating to their employees, and upward communication involves the employees communicating to their managers.

- Communication can be thought of as a five-step process.

- There are five types of communication: verbal, written modes, body language, facial expressions, and gestures.

- To determine the best way to communicate during a meeting, a person must understand that the barriers in communication are language, culture, psychological (emotional/off-limit topics), physiological (disabilities), physical, systematic (bias and politics), and attitudinal.

- Within communication, the manager assumes the roles of knowledge sharer, taskmaster, employee liaison, motivator, crisis management advisor, and stress reliever.

- The essential skills for mastering communications are understanding the context, sending multiple communications, assure the message is understood, active listening, and utilize calls to action.

- Discriminative listening involves discerning different types of sounds but not looking for any meaning in them.

- Comprehensive listening is when someone concentrates on understanding and interpreting the message being communicated.

◆ Informational listening requires listening with the goal of learning, critical listening is used to scrutinize information being delivered, and therapeutic/empathetic listening involves triggering emotion or feelings from the speaker.

◆ Active listening is when a person puts full focus and concentration on what is being said by the speaker.

Quiz

1. Which of the following is not a psychological barrier to communication?

    a. Emotional barriers

    b. Personal prejudices

    c. Hearing and speech disabilities

    d. Communication involving sensitive topics

2. Which type of communication is 'the inability to see nonverbal communication cues'?

    a. Systemic

    b. Physiological

    c. Physical

    d. Attitudinal

3. Creating a level of transparency between teams and their managers falls under which aspect of managerial communication?

    a. Motivator

    b. Employee liaison

    c. Stress reliever

    d. Task master

4. Which of the following is not true about 'Discriminative Listening'

    a. It is the earliest form of listening

    b. It helps to gather insight into nonverbal cues

    c. In combination with the visual sense, this skill helps to understand body language better

    d. It keeps developing as a person's knowledge, vocabulary, and language skills grow

5. Which category of listening will nonverbal cues such as smiling, eye contact, leaning forward, mirroring, and avoidance distractions fall into?

    a. Active listening

    b. Appreciative listening

    c. Rapport listening

    d. Emphatic listening

| **Answers** | 1 – c | 2 – c | 3 – b | 4 – d | 5 – a |

This page is intentionally left blank

Chapter 12

Change

Change is inevitable. Most organizations today are constantly changing to keep up with their industries. Change affects people, specifically, the people you manage so it is vitally important to support them through changes that occur.

Key learning objectives of this chapter include the reader's understanding of the following:

- Stages the people in an organization go through to get used to change
- Change management plan
- Change management tools

Before we go into how you can support people through change, let's take a moment to understand how people deal with change.

According to renowned psychiatrist Elisabeth Kubler-Ross, there are four stages that people go through while they are getting used to a change. These stages are referred to as the **Change Curve.**

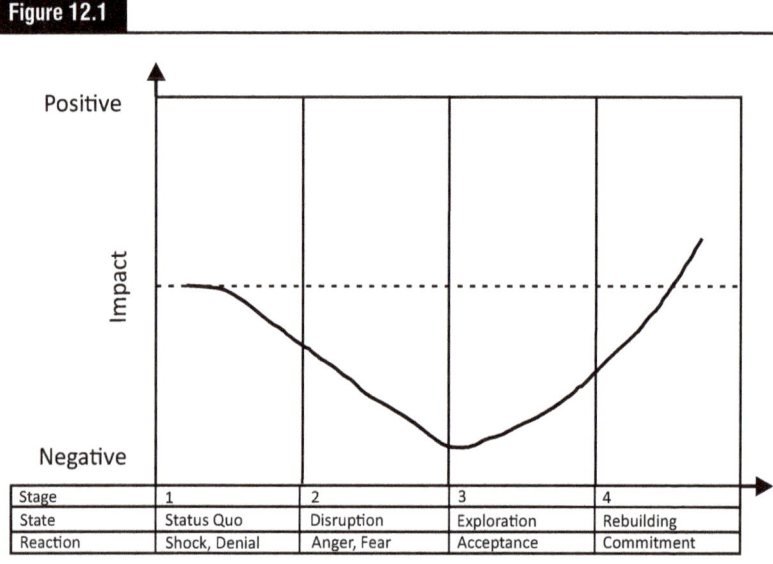

Figure 12.1

Stage	1	2	3	4
State	Status Quo	Disruption	Exploration	Rebuilding
Reaction	Shock, Denial	Anger, Fear	Acceptance	Commitment

In the first stage, a person's initial reaction is shock or denial. They realize that the change everyone has been talking about is actually happening. People need to know what is happening and know where to go to get assistance. Communication is key at this stage. Be cognizant of how much you communicate because people can easily become overwhelmed. Find the right communication balance for your organization and then make sure employees know where they can go to get more information when they need it.

In the second stage, the status quo is disrupted, and reaction begins to change to anger and fear. Resistance to the proposed change builds as personnel express their feelings or let out their anger. This stage can last for a while. If not managed properly, the implementation of the change will not be successful and the organization can go into crisis mode. Planning and preparation are key for keeping things under control. A thorough examination of the change and its impacts, with a plan to prevent possible issues, can assist in managing this stage. Regular communication upward and downward will also help mitigate the risks. Encourage employees to share any issues or concerns and provide feedback and action.

When the third stage comes about, the person is in an exploration state and the environment becomes healthier. They have begun to accept the change and become more optimistic about the future. People put behind them what they have lost during the change and begin to figure out what the change means to them. Team members will need support while they explore and test the changes. Encourage them to continue their exploration and give them the time to do it. Training is particularly important in this stage to ensure employees can cope with new processes and procedures. This stage will often see reduced productivity, but it is crucial to maintain employee buy in.

Finally, at stage four, the change is not just accepted, it is embraced. New ways of working are constructed. This stage realizes benefits the organization hoped to see when the change was proposed. People are completely used to the change and even have found it improves their work. At this last stage, celebrate the success of the implementation of the change and all you have been through.

12.1 Change Management Plan

A change management plan prepares your personnel for change. A change management plan makes the change as smooth and seamless as possible and guides employees through each step of the change. The highest risk to any change implementation is employee attitude. Poor employee attitude can affect productivity and customer satisfaction. An effective change management plan will include the following steps to help avoid this pitfall.

Define

- Define what the change looks like and how it is aligned with your organization's goals.
- Answer the questions, "what is the change needed?" and "why is this change needed?"

Impact

- Clarify who will be impacted or affected by the change.
- Answer the questions, "what is the impact?", "who is impacted?", "what are some likely concerns that those impacted will have?"

Communicate

- Construct a solid communication strategy.
- Answer the questions, "how will the change be communicated?" and "what will be done with the feedback?"

Train

- Train your team for the changes that will be implemented.
- Answer the questions, "what skills or behaviors are needed for this change?" and "how will training be delivered?"

Support

- Ensure there is a support structure in place to help those impacted and affected.
- Answer the questions, "who needs the most support?" and "what type of support is needed?"

Measure

- Measure the impact of the changes put into place.
- Answer the questions, "did the change achieve the desired goal?", "was the change management process itself effective?", and "what are the lessons learned?"

Defining the change is the first step in the change management process. This step gives context to those affected by the change. Employees want to know why the change is needed, what brought about the change, and how it will affect them. Communicate the answers to these questions clearly and concisely in order to obtain buy in. Be honest with employees and encourage them to ask questions for clarification.

The next step is to determine who will be impacted. This task can sometimes be overlooked. We can easily identify the areas that will be directly impacted by the change, but what about the areas indirectly impacted? For example, a factory producing widgets has decided to change out part A to part B because the technology of part B is more up to date and sophisticated. We can say the department that installs part A will be directly impacted. What about the downstream areas installing parts configured to work with the old part A? Those areas will be impacted too. All areas impacted need to know how they will be affected and the possible issues they may encounter.

Communication, in any process, is the most important part. If a change is implemented but not communicated effectively, the success of the implementation will be negatively impacted. Employee morale will suffer. Ensure that there are several modes of communication for your audience including those who may not have ready access to a computer, work third shift, or have a flexible schedule.

Training helps the people affected deal appropriately with the change. If a new widget is to be used, employees need to know how to install the new widget. Again, you want to make sure that you offer training that can work for every employee. You may need to offer several modes of training such as a computer-based, in class, and self-study training. When developing the training plan, be sure to document what training needs to take place and how it will be delivered.

As the change is being implemented, a strong support structure needs to be in place for employees who need help. The support team can answer questions and address concerns that could be related to training, implementation issues, or the change itself. When determining the support structure, identify who will need the support and what types of support may be appropriate. For example, an area that is not largely impacted by the change would not benefit as much from an onsite support staff person as an area that is greatly impacted.

Finally, measure how the implementation of the change went. Was it successful? In order to answer this question, you need to make sure you have a defined measurable goal and a baseline to measure to. This reporting will not only tell you if your change was successful but can also indicate any issues that are coming up. At the end of any change document your lessons learned. Essentially you ask, what went wrong, was it preventable, and how would we plan for it in future projects?

12.2 Change Management Tools

Several tools have been developed to assist organizations through change. Although all of them cannot be discussed in their entirety in this section, the following list includes a brief summary of tools you may find useful. You are encouraged to seek out additional resources for more information on these tools.

- **Understanding the Change**
    - **The Change Curve** – Briefly discussed earlier in this section, this tool helps you understand the stages a person goes through when they are adjusting to change. Using this tool will assist you in better understanding the change so you may take this into consideration while planning.
    - **Lewin's Change Management Model** – This helps you understand how breaking up the current state is needed to really implement and see improvement. This model uses a concept called

"unfreeze-change-refreeze" to describe how this can be done.

- **Beckhard and Harris's Change Model** – This model looks at change from a different vantage point. It suggests people have to be dissatisfied with the current state and develop a picture of how the change implemented in a future state would be better. This coupled with the knowledge of how to get to that ideal future state ensures the implementation of the change will be successful.

- Planning Change

  - **Impact Analysis** – This analysis allows you to fully examine all consequences of change, especially the unexpected consequences.

  - **Burke-Litwin Change Model** – This model takes 12 elements of organizational design to help you walk through the effects of the change.

  - **McKinsey 7S Framework** – A popular tool widely used, this looks at the seven "hard" and "soft" characteristics of an organization to understand their relationships to the change.

  - **Leavitt's Diamond** – This tool is similar to the two earlier discussed tools in that it looks at impacts of change on the tasks, people, structure, and technology in an organization while taking their relationships into account.

  - **Organization Design** – This tool discussed in an earlier section references the more common structures of organizational design, so you can develop the best design for your organization.

- **SIPOC Diagrams** – SIPOC stands for suppliers, inputs, processes, outputs, and customers. This tool looks at the impact on these elements as a result of the change.

- **Implementing Change**

  - **Kotter's 8-Step Change Model** – This model outlines what activities need to be done to effect change permanently.

  - **Training Needs Assessment** – This assessment helps ensure the right training is delivered to the right staff at the appropriate time.

  - **Why Change Can Fail** – As you may now have inferred, change is complicated. Learn from others' mistakes with this tool.

- **Communicating Change**

  - **Stakeholder Analysis** – A great way to discover who your project's stakeholders are, prioritizing how they are affected, and understanding their needs.

  - **Stakeholder Management** – The next step in the process of working with your stakeholders, this allows you to put a plan in place to communicate the right message the first time to the right stakeholder. If done effectively, you will get the support you need from the parties involved.

- **Mission and Vision Statements** – These statements help you to communicate the reason for the change, how it aligns with organizational mission and vision, and help to encourage enthusiasm for an improved future state.

Chapter Summary

- The change curve illustrates the stages that occur when someone is getting used to change. These stages are status quo, disruption, exploration, and rebuilding.

- The reactions are shock/denial, anger/fear, acceptance, and commitment respectively.

- A change management plan is used to make the change as smooth and seamless as possible. The six steps to developing this plan are defining, impact, communication, train, support, and measure.

- The key tools for understanding the change are the change curve, Lewin's change management model, and Beckhard/Harris's change model.

- The key tools for planning change are the impact analysis, Burke-Litwin change model, McKinsey 7S framework, Levitt's diamond, organization design, and SIPOC diagrams.

- The key tools for implementing change are Kotter's 8-Step change model, training needs assessment, and understanding why change can fail.

- The key tools for communicating change are the stakeholder analysis, stakeholder management tactics, and the mission/vision statements.

Quiz

1. Which of the following options reflects the correct sequence of stages of reaction to change
   i. Anger and fear
   ii. Optimistic about the future
   iii. Shock and denial
   iv. Realization of benefits

   a. (C → A → B → D)
   b. (A → B → C → D)
   c. (D → C → B → A)
   d. (B → A → C → D)

2. Which of the following statements is incorrect?

   a. The highest risk to change implementation is employee attitude
   b. In the exploration stage, the organizational environment becomes confused
   c. People need to know what is happening and where to get assistance when they are in a shock and denial mood.
   d. Poor employee attitude can affect productivity and customer satisfaction

3. 'The change curve', 'Lewin's Change Management model', 'Beckhard and Harris's Change Model' are used for

   a. Planning change

   b. Understanding change

   c. Implementing change

   d. Communicating change

4. Which of the following is a wrong statement?

   a. Burke-Litwin Change model takes 12 elements of organizational design

   b. Leavitt's Diamond looks at the impact of Change on tasks, people, structure, and Technology

   c. SIPOC stands for Strength, Innovation, Productivity, Opportunity, and Collaboration

   d. Mckinsey's 7S Framework looks at seven 'soft 'and 'hard' characteristics of an organization

5. Stakeholder analysis, Stakeholder management, mission ,and vision statements are related to:

   a. Planning change

   b. Understanding change

   c. Implementing change

   d. Communicating change

| Answers | 1 – a | 2 – b | 3 – b | 4 – c | 5 – d |

This page is intentionally left blank

Chapter 13

Organizational Culture

Organizational culture is the lifeblood of an organization. Each organization has its own individual culture. Culture plays a large part in all the activities we have discussed. Management style and leadership style will only be effective in an organization if they are in alignment with its culture. Communications will be successful only if it is aligned culturally. Teams can be more effective in building processes if they consider the culture.

Key learning objectives of this chapter include the reader's understanding of the following:

- Types of organizational cultures
- The factors that influence cultures
- Disadvantages of culture
- Open door policy

The values, beliefs and principles of an organization comprise the organization's culture. The organization's culture has a huge impact on the employees as well as their relationships internally. Employee success is dependent upon a clear understanding of the organization's unique culture.

In the most general sense, there are two types of organizational culture – strong and weak. In a strong culture, employees enjoy coming to work every day. They look forward to new assignments and new challenges. They follow established policies and procedures embrace their roles and responsibilities.

In a weak culture, employees complete their roles and responsibilities out of fear of leadership. They go to work every day because they need the money. They do not enjoy their work and often feel compelled to do things required by management rather than out of internal motivation to better the organization. Employees do not have loyalty to this organization and therefore present a greater risk of increased attrition.

13.1 Specific Types of Organizational Culture

As we break down organizational cultures, we find there are several more specific types of cultures that organizations can be categorized into. The following is a list of the more commonly seen types:

- **Normative** – Employees express ideal behaviors in that they strictly follow policies and procedures of the organization. Employees do not consider breaking the rules and therefore stick to what the organization has outlined. The norms and procedures of the organization have been well defined and set from existing guidelines.

- **Pragmatic** – The customer is king is a key phrase of this culture. Emphasis is placed on customers and ensuring their satisfaction. Employees are driven to client satisfaction as their main goal and therefore do not feel compelled to follow any set of rules.

- **Academy** – Training is a central focus. Recruiters search for skilled workers to add to the team. Background, experience, and education dictate how work is delegated. Internally, knowledge and training programs for existing employees are well invested in. Leadership genuinely wants to see the knowledge of their employees expand so they can excel in their career. This culture fosters longer employee working relationships because they are continuously growing within. This culture is common in schools, universities, and healthcare facilities.

- **Baseball team** – This culture recognizes the real value of the employee. They understand the employee is vital to the successful functioning of the organization. The scales of power tend to tip in the direction of the employee, and this increases the risk of them taking advantage of that power. Financial organizations, event management, and advertising industry organizations typically have this culture.

- **Club** – This culture runs more like the organization is an exclusive club you want to join. They recruit only the best in their area and are looking for specific specialties, education, and interests. Employees with the most potential are more likely to be promoted. Appraisals are also often used.

- **Fortress** – There is a constant state of uncertainty in a fortress culture. Employees are uncertain about the stability of their jobs and careers. If the organization does not perform as expected, employees can be terminated. When the organization performs poorly, employees suffer the most. You see this culture in stock broking organizations.

- **Tough guy** – This culture may be categorized as micromanaging since employees are always under close surveillance. Feedbacks are prevalent, and performance is regularly reviewed. Work is monitored, and team leaders communicate with team members regarding needed improvements.

- **Bet your company** – This culture takes on a lot of risk even if the possible results are unable to be foreseen. Policies and procedures are built to address the most sensitive issues. Results are not seen quickly in this organization.

- **Process** – These organizations are guided by policies and procedures. Everything has a policy that is adhered to. Feedbacks and performance reviews are less important than whether the rules and regulations were followed. Government organizations typically operate under this culture.

13.2 Importance of Culture

We know culture affects everything downstream in an established organization. What about at the onset of an organization? What makes culture important? Let's examine the following outlined reasons for its importance.

- Employees interact with one another according to culture. If the culture is healthy, employees are loyal and respectful to management and the organization.

- Healthy competition can be encouraged with the right culture. With the spirit of healthy competition, employees work to outperform each other with their own internal motivation.

- The culture acts as a guide for employees, giving them a sense of direction with predefined policies.

- The culture gives the organization an identity which lends to the organization's brand image.

- The culture brings employees together to a common ground.

- Culture can unite diverse employee populations.

- The right culture promotes strong relationships amongst its employees.

- Culture can be the instigator to encourage employees to perform to their fullest potential.

13.3 What Influences Culture?

During your career, you may hear someone say, "Does he/she fit well with our culture?" Culture drives many things in an organization, so you always want to ask this question when hiring new people. How do you tell if the person is a fit? Some people may go by a gut feeling but there are some identified factors that influence culture that you can look at.

- Each individual affects the culture of an organization. Attitudes, personalities, values, and beliefs of an individual can positively or negatively contribute to the whole.

- Employee sex affects culture. For example, if an organization is female dominated, more emphasis may be placed on employee emotional wellbeing and feelings.

- The nature of the business itself dictates part of the culture. Industries highly affected by external factors may have a significantly different culture than a hospital. This difference could be attributed to the dependency on market performance.

- Goals and objectives stated by the organization guide the culture as well. For example, financial trading organizations expect their employees to be able to deal with stressful situations and a fast-paced environment. A healthcare system expects their employees to be caring, compassionate and patient.

- Since the organization cannot live and breathe without clients, the culture is naturally affected by their demands. A company that services overseas clients may have to work off hours according to the client schedule.

- Management and other leadership have a strong influence on culture. They set the tone. If micro-managed, employees may frequently request input on daily work activities and work less autonomously.

Time influences culture. As time passes by, people and environment changes. These changes can cause the culture to evolve. A recent example of this is the entry of the millennials into the workplace. That generation is highly influenced by technology. This has influenced flexible work schedules at many organizations. A culture once driven by socialization in person at work has now evolved into socializing via instant messaging, email, and video conferencing. Common reasons for culture changes are new management or leadership, financial changes, external factors, and a change in the target customer population.

13.4 Disadvantages of Culture

Organizational culture does have its disadvantages you need to consider. Identifying these disadvantages allows you to plan on how to minimize the impact when they occur.

- Culture is formed over a period of time. In the same respect, cultural changes do not happen overnight. It is a lengthy process.

- If you are not hiring people that fit your culture, the adjustment process can be particularly difficult. This also increases the risk of higher training costs due to attrition.

- Some cultures become more of a hindrance than a help. If the culture of your organization imposes harsh rules and guidelines, you may find it difficult to retain employees for any length of time.

- Some cultures are unchanging and stick to the status quo. They do not flex with the environment and therefore do not foster innovation. Your ability to sustain your organization's place in the industry and attract new talent may be threatened.

- Cultures should not become more important than the employee.

13.5 Open Door Policy

The "open door policy" has become a common facet of many organizational cultures. Undoubtedly you have heard a leader say, "I have an open-door policy." The purpose of this policy is to have complete transparency at all levels of the organization. Leadership's doors are open to any employee, regardless of their position in the organization, to ask questions or voice concerns. This policy was developed in response to an environment where employees had to use their "chain of command". They could only go to their direct manager with their questions. This bred distrust of leadership amongst the employees and affected employee morale.

With the open-door policy open communication is highly encouraged throughout all ranks of the organization. With the increased transparency, employees become more loyal to leadership and managers. Exchanging ideas and asking questions that are constructive are promoted. Relationships are fostered between managers and their subordinates allowing employees a level of comfort in approaching their leaders with questions or for clarity. Fearing your superior is a thing of the past.

Chapter Summary

- Organizational culture is comprised of the values, beliefs, and principles of an organization.

- Normative culture allows employees to express ideal behaviors due to strict policies and procedures.

- Pragmatic culture causes the emphasis to be placed on ensuring customer satisfaction.

- Academy culture requires recruiters to add skilled workers based on talent and training.

- A baseball team culture focuses on the employees and their satisfaction within the organization.

- Club culture presents an exclusive vibe due to recruiting the best available in specific areas.

- The fortress culture causes uncertainty regarding the stability of an employee's job and career.

- The tough guys culture is centered around micromanaging employees.

- The bet your company culture brings high risk without identifying foreseen results.

- Process culture is guided by policies and procedures.

- Culture is important because of the direct effect on how employees interact, the status of healthy competition within the organization, establishing guidance to policies, giving the organization an identity, uniting diversity within an organization, promoting strong relationships, and can encourage employees to perform to their fullest potential.

◆ Culture is influenced by each individual, the employee demographic, the nature of the business, the goals and objectives established by the organization, client demand levels, and management/other leadership.

Quiz

1. Which of the following statements is wrong?

    a. There are three broader types of cultures: good, bad, and mixed

    b. There are two broader types of cultures: strong and weak

    c. Employees enjoy coming to work every day if the culture of the organization is strong

    d. Employees do not have loyalty toward an organization that has a weak culture.

2. Which of the pair of organizational culture types is erroneously described?

    a. Normative – The employees express ideal behavior

    b. Pragmatic – The customer is the King

    c. Academy – Training is the central focus

    d. Baseball Team – Employees are sports savvy

3. Policies and procedures are built to address the most sensitive issues in which type of organizational culture?

    a. Process

    b. Bet your company

    c. Tough guy

    d. Fortress

4. Which of the pair is wrongly described?

   a. Management and other leadership – They set the tone

   b. Goals and objectives – Healthcare system employees are expected to be compassionate

   c. Employee sex – Emphasis on emotional well-being

   d. Time – The employees are time conscious and work only for stipulated hours

5. Which of the following is right?

   a. Cultural changes do not happen overnight

   b. Harsh rules and guidelines help in the retention of employees

   c. The adjustment process is easier for people not fitting with the culture

   d. Rigid culture and sticking to the status quo enables innovation

| **Answers** | 1 – a | 2 – d | 3 – b | 4 – d | 5 – a |

Chapter 14

Total Quality Management

Total Quality Management (TQM) is the continuous effort by management to improve processes in order to produce the highest quality product or service. The purpose of this exercise is to ensure long term loyalty from customers. Managers have a leading role in TQM because they are the initiators of the process and implement the changes.

Key learning objectives of this chapter include the reader's understanding of the following:

- Four stages of TQM
- Eight aspects of TQM
- Main tools to facilitate the implementation of TQM
- Major role of TQM in production and operations management

Quality is the parameter that determines whether a product or service is excellent or poor. Durability, ease of use, reliability, versatility, etc. are examples of parameters commonly used to describe the quality of a product or service. Quality distinguishes you from the competitor and keeps the customer purchasing from you.

TQM gives every employee a part in the process of ensuring a superior product or service. Each employee is encouraged to work towards improving the work culture, processes, systems and all other aspects that go into producing the product or service.

TQM is an important process because it ensures many things that contribute to the stability of your organization. It ensures that your organization is producing the highest quality product every time. It encourages customer loyalty, satisfaction and longevity. TQM guides the organization in creating a product that the customer actually wants to purchase. Putting the changes into place from TQM can increase revenues and ensure greater productivity. Total Quality Management also helps to reduce waste and standing inventory.

TQM has four stages:

- Plan
- Do
- Check
- Act

Figure 14.1

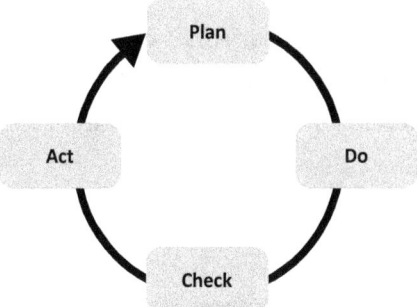

14.1 Plan

This stage begins the process and is arguably the most important. Employees must identify the issue to be addressed accurately and thoroughly. They may gather these issues from their own day to day procedures or customer feedback. At this point, the employees investigate to find the root cause and research to find all possible solutions.

14.2 Do

At this point, the employees take the solution they selected in the plan phase and implement it. They develop an implementation strategy to guide the implementation and measure the success of the solution.

14.3 Check

During this stage, a comparison is completed of the previous current state and the current state with the implemented solution. The effectiveness of the process and the results are measured.

14.4 Act

During the act stage, document the results and identify any new issues to be addressed. Examine your findings and take action. If the change you implemented was successful, see if there is a way to incorporate the positive change into a wider area. If the change was unsuccessful, test again with a different change.

14.5 Aspects of TQM

Ensuring TQM is implemented correctly requires several different elements. If your implementation is missing one of these elements, it will fail. These aspects include:

- Communication
- Ethics
- Recognition
- Integrity
- Teamwork
- Leadership

- Trust
- Training

Figure 14.2

Ethics, integrity and trust are the foundation of TQM. At its very core, you must have these elements to be successful. As you move away from the core, training, teamwork and leadership become increasingly important. These elements make up the structure of the TQM. Communication brings it all together. Communication flowing in all directions allows the TQM elements to function in place. The most important piece is recognition. Recognition is the driver that keeps the TQM model going. It motivates employees to work hard and always strive for better.

14.6 TQM Tools

As you work to implement TQM in your organization, you need to be aware of various tools that are helpful in facilitating this work. Let's take a look at these tools and their functions.

- **Checklist** – This is an easy way to collect data. Utilize the checklist to list the problems identified. Once a solution has been determined, check the item off the list.
    - Defect in Widget A
    - Not enough staffing at the loading dock
    - No double-check process in place
    - Broken piece in machine B
- **Pareto Chart** – Vilfredo Pareto developed the Pareto Chart to aid in identifying and prioritizing problems as well as track their frequency. It is a pictorial way of identifying the defects and how often they happen in the system, so the employee can attack the most commonly occurring issues first.

Figure 14.3

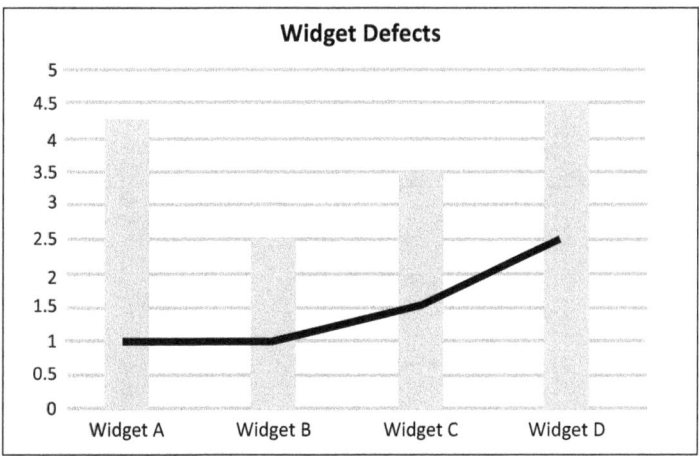

- **Cause and Effect Diagram** – This tool is also known as a fishbone diagram. This tool is used to help you find the root cause of a problem by diagramming all the causes.

Figure 14.4

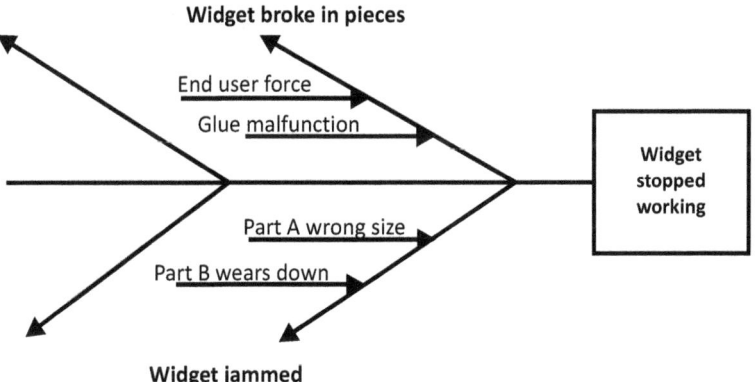

- **Histogram** – This tool was developed by Karl Pearson. The tool shows a picture of the intensity of the problem. You can see this with the shape and width of the distribution.

Figure 14.5

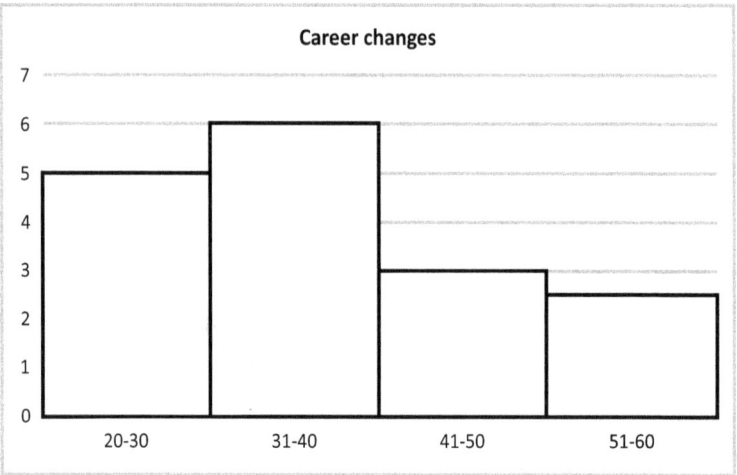

- **Scatter Diagram** – This diagram looks at the relationship between two variables. Data is shown as points on the diagram and a cluster of points means there is a relationship between the two variables.

Figure 14.6

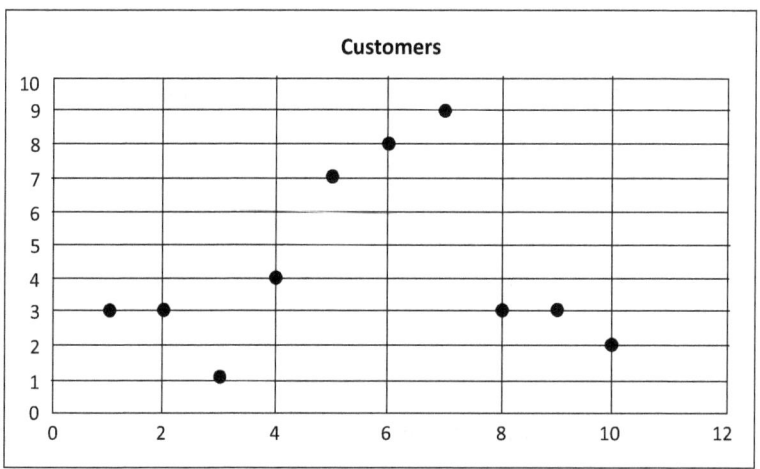

- **Graphs** – Graphs are the easiest and most common TQM tool used. They help to tell you if a process is performing to the expected level and if there are any major deviations in that process.

Figure 14.7

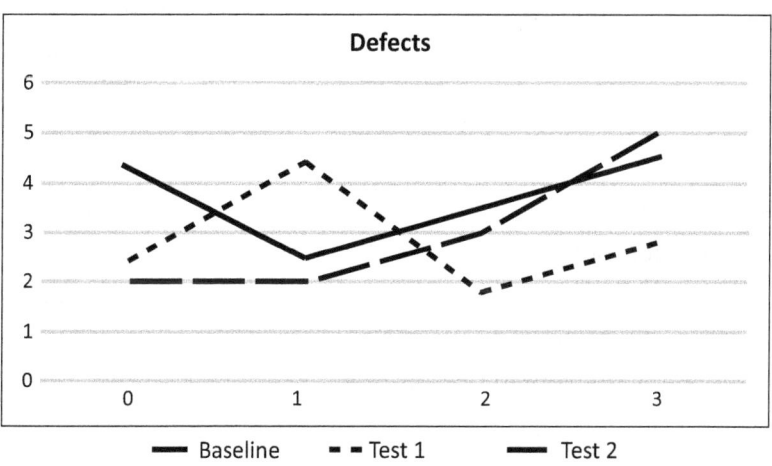

14.7 Production vs. Operations Management

Production and operations management is the management of the day to day activities of the organization. Production is the process of turning raw materials into a finished product with economic value to sell to a customer. Production is completed three ways:

- **Production through separation** – The desired product is produced when you extract a piece from the raw material.

- **Production through improvement** – The desired product is produced when the chemical or mechanical properties are modified without modifying it physically.

- **Production by assembly** – The desired product is produced when pieces are put together to make a whole product. Production management is important because the outputs affect the customer directly and therefore the fate of the organization as well. An efficiently and effectively managed production line can keep costs low while building superior products to deliver to the customers. This builds customer satisfaction and loyalty.

Operations management guides the company in identifying the customer's needs and ensures a product or service meeting their needs is produced. Operations management allows you to look at a finished product and backwards engineer the raw materials needed to create the product. It also includes collaborating with vendors, both internal and external, to obtain the materials needed for successful delivery to the consumer.

Although production and operations management seem similar, they are distinct entities of their own. The following list details their major differences:

- The outputs of production management are solely the manufacturing of products. The outputs of operations management can be either products or services or both.

- A product can only be used over a period of time until it begins to depreciate and become unusable. A service has to be utilized immediately.

- Production of products requires more capital investment and less labor. Services are just the opposite where there is larger labor investment and less capital investment.

- There is no direct contact with the customer in the production of a product. When delivering services, customer contact is constant.

Chapter Summary

- Total Quality Management is the continuous effort by management to improve processes in order to produce the highest quality product or service and ensure long term loyalty from customers.

- TQM ensures that the many aspects of the organization contribute to the overall stability through four stages: Plan, Do (implement the solution), Check and Act.

- The various aspects of TQM are communication, ethics, recognition, integrity, teamwork, leadership, trust, and training.

- Key tools for TQM are checklists, Pareto charts (identify, prioritize, and track problems), cause and effect diagrams, histograms, scatter diagrams, and comparison graphs.

- Production is the process of turning raw materials into a finished good with economic value.

- Operations management guides the company in identifying the customer's needs and ensuring that a product or service is produced to meet their needs.

Quiz

1. **Which of the following statements is wrong?**

    a. TQM contributes to the stability of any organization

    b. TQM enlists every employee's participation in the process

    c. Managers have a very minimal role in TQM

    d. TQM guides the organization in creating a product or service which the customer actually wants

2. **Pertaining to the four important stages of TQM, which statement is wrong?**

    a. Plan: The employees identify the issue accurately and thoroughly

    b. Do: The implementation strategy is developed

    c. Check: The effectiveness of the process and the results are measured

    d. Act: If the change implemented is unsuccessful, the entire TQM activity is to be dropped by the organization

3. **_____ brings all together and flowing in all directions**

    a. Ethics, integrity, and trust

    b. Training, teamwork, and leadership

    c. Recognition

    d. Communication

4. 'The shape and width of the distribution reveals the intensity of the problem'. Which TQM tool is this?

   a. Pareto chart

   b. Fishbone diagram

   c. Histogram

   d. Scatter diagram

5. Which of the following statements is wrong?

   a. A product can be used over a period of time until it begins to depreciate and become unusable

   b. Production of products requires more capital investment and labor

   c. The outputs of operations management are solely products.

   d. There is no direct contact with the customer in the production of a product

| **Answers** | 1 – c | 2 – d | 3 – d | 4 – c | 5 – c |

Chapter 15

Operations

There must be an operational strategy that ties to the overall objective of the company. This strategy will establish an operational goal that will guide the day to day operations. With the external environment always changing, the goals and strategies need to be nimble, so they can change to the market demand.

Key learning objectives of this chapter include the reader's understanding of the following:

- Steps to build a business strategy
- Role of technology to customize the design of products and services.

Figure 15.1

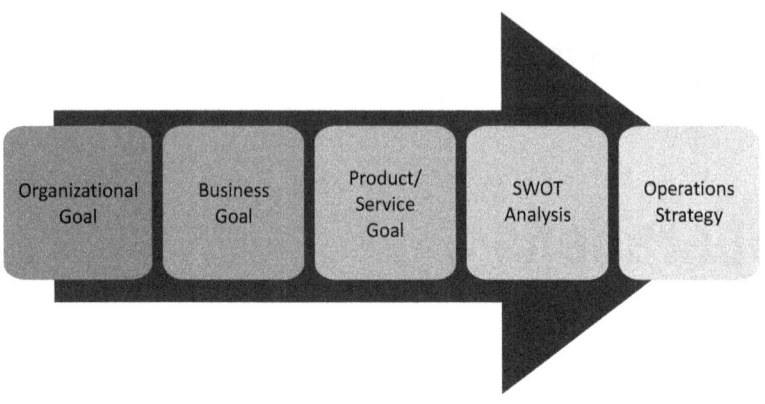

Building strategy is a process that flows down through an organization. Various steps need to be accomplished to ensure all business functions have been accounted for.

- **Competitive analysis** – What does the current competition look like? What processes are they utilizing in their production and operations to be most efficient? What is the industry standard?

- **Goal setting** – The organization decides the end goal we will work towards.

- **Build strategy** – How will we accomplish this goal through production and operations?

- **Implementation** – Implement in our day to day activities the production and operations strategies determined in the step above.

After these steps are followed, it will be a continuous process to measure productivity and performance to the goals determined. Not only will you measure whether you are meeting the goal, but you also want to measure whether you are utilizing your capital and labor resources most efficiently. While you are monitoring this performance, you will note areas for improvement and put into place revisions to hopefully close the gaps.

Another indicator of our success is a measurement of how much we are wasting. When we look at the raw material that goes into the production of the product, how much of that raw material is wasted in production? Is there a way to better utilize that raw material? Examples of waste are producing defects, idle machine time, and idle labor time.

15.1 Role of Technology

Technology plays a large role in today's business environment. Managing technology in operations management is a role in itself. Technology has a huge impact on productivity and waste. Technology's role in operations management continues to evolve as technology becomes more advanced. In the current environment, when we reference technology as part of operations management, it includes the design and development of products, as well as managing and improving upon current operations processes.

Technology is a vital part of increasing productivity and improving effectiveness in any production system. When you choose to bring in technology, it is helpful to consider the following things.

- **Acquisition** – When acquiring technology, a thorough cost- benefit analysis should be completed and there should be a clear alignment with organizational goals and objectives.

- **Integration** – An integration plan should be constructed to help integrate the new technology. This plan should consider the technology's effect on each business system.

- **Validation** – After the technology has been integrated, there should be an ongoing process to validate that the technology is doing what you expect it to do.

Technology has been used increasingly more in manufacturing industries. The technology allows businesses to customize the design of product and services. Below are common methods used at the current time:

- **Computer Aided Design (CAD)** – CAD uses computer software to create detailed two dimensional and three-dimensional designs and models. It is commonly used by architects, engineers, and artists.

- **Computer Aided Manufacturing System (CAM)** – CAM uses computer software and machinery to automate and expedite manufacturing practices.

- **Computer Aided Engineering (CAE)** – CAE uses computer software to assist in engineering examination activities.

- **Standard for the Exchange of Product Data** – This is a neutral file exchange used in CAM to share the product information across all phases of the life cycle.

Although technology has proven to be a great help in the manufacturing industry as well as others, there are some issues with the use of technology. Technology does require a high investment and maintaining its functionality is costly as well. Technology can very easily be mismanaged if you do not have qualified people working on it.

Chapter Summary

- To assure all business functions are accounted for in developing an operational strategy, organizations should conduct a competitive analysis, set goals for organization, build their strategy based on goals, and then implement the strategy.

- Technology has a major impact on productivity and waste, and organizations should consider acquisitions, integration, and validation of technology before implementation.

- Businesses use various products such as CAD, CAM, CAE, and Standard for the Exchange of Product Data to customize the design of products.

Quiz

1. _____ is useful to share the product information across all phases of the life cycle of a computer software used to create designs and models

   a. Computer-Aided Design (CAD)

   b. Computer Aided Manufacturing System (CAM)

   c. Computer Aided Engineering (CAE)

   d. Standard for the Exchange of Product Data (SEPD)

2. Which of the following is wrong?

   a. Competitive analysis talks about the process utilized by competitors to be more efficient

   b. Goal setting talks about the end goal an organization works towards

   c. Building strategy talks about how to accomplish the goal through production and operations

   d. Implementation talks about the implementation of the production and operation strategies in our quarterly activities

3. Which of the following is a correct statement?

   a. Technology is a vital part of increasing productivity and improving effectiveness in any production system

   b. When acquiring technology, cost-benefit analysis is the last priority

c. Integration plan need not take into consideration technology's effect on business systems

d. Validation is not an ongoing process that the technology is performing as per expectation

4. _____ is commonly used by architects, engineers, and artists.

   a. Computer-Aided Design (CAD)

   b. Computer Aided Manufacturing System (CAM)

   c. Computer Aided Engineering(CAE)

   d. The standard for the Exchange of Product Data(SEPD)

5. Which of the following is in the right order for the operational strategy that ties the overall objective of the company?

   a. Organizational Goal → Product/Service Goal → SWOT Analysis → Business Goal → Operations Strategy

   b. Organizational Goal → Business Goal → Product/Service Goal → SWOT Analysis → Operations Strategy

   c. Organizational Goal → SWOT Analysis → Product/Service Goal → Business Goal → Operations Strategy

   d. Organizational Goal → SWOT Analysis → Business Goal → Product/Service Goal → Operations Strategy

| **Answers** | 1 – d | 2 – d | 3 – a | 4 – a | 5 – b |

Chapter 16

People Management

As a manager the largest role you play is in people management. Your largest and most challenging job is obtaining, utilizing and retaining a team of people who are satisfied with their jobs. This is quite an undertaking so understanding all the elements involved is crucial to your success.

As a manager of people, you will have support from your Human Resources liaison. Your human resources liaison is responsible for supporting leaders, guiding line managers regarding personnel questions and challenges, counseling employees on grievances and problems, mediating between employees and managers, and being the voice of the employees and the organization itself.

Key learning objectives of this chapter include the reader's understanding of the following:

- Staffing process

- Staffing challenges
- Orientation of employees to their specific job responsibilities and expectations
- Objectives and benefits of designing a performance management plan
- Steps involved in the preparation of an effective performance management plan for the employees of the organization

The work of a human resources or personnel manager can be categorized into four main functions:

- Planning for staffing
- Recruiting new talent
- Selecting appropriate candidates
- Developing and training new employees

Manpower planning (human resources planning or staffing planning) is when you estimate the optimal level of staffing required for a project, task, or goal. Planning considers not just how many people are needed, but also what skillsets are needed, when they are needed, and how long they are needed for. This requires looking at your own internal resources to see if there are needs due to employees transferring or leaving as well as considering if there are any skillsets in house that may fit the needs you are looking for.

People Management

Figure 16.1

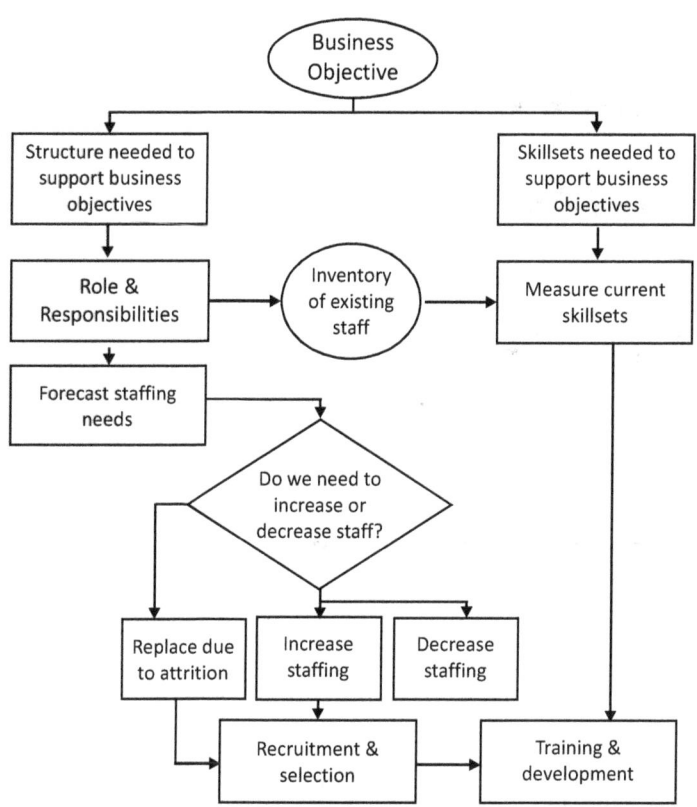

16.1 Staffing Process

After determining you have a staffing need, you need to acquire the staffing and make sure they are ready to work. The process does not stop there. You also want to make sure you are doing all the appropriate activities to retain that person.

- **Approval** – Define the role and skillset needed. Acquire approval and funding for the position to be filled by appropriate leadership.

- **Recruiting** – Advertise the vacancy and solicit applications.

- **Selection** – Screen candidates according to skillset and fit through review of resumes and interviews. Present an offer to the desired candidate.

- **Orientation** – When a candidate accepts the offer, he or she becomes familiar with their new work environment and teams through orientation. At this point, you are placing the right person in the right position.

- **Training and development** – Initial training prepares the person for their new role. Training is continuously offered to encourage growth and development of that employee. Training gives employees a deeper knowledge of their specialty area and, if they choose, knowledge of other related areas.

- **Remuneration** – This type of compensation is monetary and is provided as an incentive to employees. This is often related to work performance, skillset, etc

- **Performance evaluation** – Performance evaluations should be prepared at regular intervals throughout an employee's tenure at an organization. The purpose of evaluations is to keep the employee informed and to maintain documentation regarding the employee's performance, behaviors, etc. It helps the employee and the manager see how the employee's skillset is developing and where additional training may be needed for promotion to the next level.

- **Promotion and transfer** – Promotions occur when an employee is shifted to a position considered a higher level than his/her current role. This role typically has more demands and responsibilities. Transfers are when employees choose to shift to different departments or branches in the same organization.

16.2 Staffing Challenges

Human resources planning is one of the costliest processes in an organization. If an organization can reduce its attrition, it can reduce costs. Understanding the challenges of manpower planning will help us to better plan to obtain the right team members and retain them.

- Manpower should be utilized to its optimal capacity. Look at the skill sets of your employees and ensure they are in the right positions. Does it make sense at your organization to have a person with 5 years industry experience and a bachelor's degree in an entry level position? Are you fully utilizing that resource's skillset? It is easier to move a highly skilled worker to a higher position than it is to move an unqualified person from a higher position to a lower level position.
- Absenteeism is a rising issue in the industry today. Absenteeism is defined by Dictionary.com as the practice of staying out of work for no good reason. Common causes of absenteeism are:

- Bullying and harassment
- Burnout and stress
- Dependent care
- Depression;
- Low to no engagement
- Illness
- Injury
- Looking for another job
- Partial shift attendance

- Lack of qualified employees means more unfilled positions at organizations. The skillsets and education needed for the roles are simply not available in the workplace. Attracting and maintaining the skillsets needed is a growing challenge in today's environment.

- The controlling process for acquiring and releasing manpower can be a time-consuming process. Usually, the need for a new employee has to be approved by top level leaders. Human resource plans and budgets have to be consulted and determined if this role is within the defined limitations of the planning.

- Training and development of employees to keep up with the pace of change in today's evolving environment.

- Identifying and developing leaders to rise in the organization.

- Designing and maintaining a Human Resources program in the organization that can attract and retain top talent in each generation. This includes being competitive in compensation, flexible work schedules, philanthropy, etc.

16.3 Recruiting Staff

As identified earlier, one of the biggest challenges of today is recruiting the right staff. There are several different avenues you can explore to look for candidates to fill your open positions. Let's take a closer look at some of the options available.

Looking internally at possible candidates is the first place you want to go. It is great for employee growth and morale if you can move the employee up through the ranks from within. Besides the positive aspects on the workforce, internal recruitment is less costly and requires less time and effort. The challenge of internal recruitment is locating the right employee. Often internal recruitment happens when an employee applies for an open position or a person recommends another employee for the role. What about the qualified candidates who may be interested in the role but did not apply or were not recommended? Utilizing a comprehensive human resources system to query the workforce by skillset and requirements would be ideal to locate these employees. Unfortunately, this type of technology is not widely used in organizations today.

Another option is to look externally for candidates. This involves looking outside of your organization for the right skillsets. The following are common sources of external recruitment:

- **Employment at the organization level** – This is where you post the open position on the organization bulletin board or sign outside the organization that is viewable by external applicants. This type of recruitment is typically done at factories and does not always attract the most desirable applicants.

- **Advertisements** – Posting through an external source such as want ads, on a job website, or advertising on TV. The biggest advantage to this is you reach a large amount of people with a wide variety of skillsets.

- **Employment exchanges** – An employment exchange is usually run by the government. The government collects education, experience, and other pertinent data on candidates for recruitment needs.

- **Employment agencies** – These agencies recruit people to help other organizations meet their manpower needs. These agencies vary from "headhunters" to "temp agencies." Some provide temporary employees for specific time periods, permanent employees or "temp to hire" employees.

- **Educational institutions** – Some educational institutions specialize in placing students in positions when they graduate. This type of recruitment is called Campus Recruitment. It is a great place to find a large pool of possible candidates. The disadvantage is many candidates have limited work experience.

- **Recommendations** – Word of mouth is a common way of finding candidates as well. The recommendations often come from employees familiar with the position and its needs, so some of your better candidates come from these sources.

- **Labor Contractors** – Companies provide qualified people as contractors to fill vacant positions. These people are usually contracted for a specific time period. This can be a great source to quickly find the skillset you need. The disadvantage is that these resources are typically costlier than filling the open position, and if the resource's contract is not renewed, you still have a vacancy to fill.

16.4 Selecting the Right Employee

As we learned earlier, acquiring and hiring new resources is a very costly process. Imagine the cost when you have frequent turnover due to choosing the wrong employee for the position. The U.S. Department of Labor estimates that the price of a bad hire is almost 30% of the first-year salary for the employee. It can also have effects on employee morale and team building. Take a look at some steps you can take to help ensure you choose the right candidate:

- Clearly define the job, its responsibilities and the skillset required.

- Strategize on how you will recruit the right employee. Gather together all of the resources involved in recruitment and hiring for this position to discuss the best way to meet the open role. This group may include the hiring manager, the team where the vacancy is located, and the Human Resources liaison.

- Develop a checklist for hiring employee hiring. What tasks need to be completed? What takes priority? As each item is completed, check it off the list. Keep communication flowing with all of the resources involved in the hiring process

- Consider internal applicants you or your team members have relationships with. Building a talent pool to pull resources from when you have open positions is ideal for any manager.

- Carefully review applications and credentials. Start with a preliminary review to weed out those who do not meet the minimum eligibility requirements. Review the resumes and applications provided to determine if they meet the minimum requirements. Typically, your Human Resources recruitment resource will assist you in doing this. Next, have a list of your top desirable skills and characteristics of the right individual for the role and look for candidates that match.

- Conduct prescreening interviews. The purpose of the prescreening interview is to utilize the interview team's time most efficiently and effectively by ruling out inappropriate candidates for interviews. Have a list of questions prepared for this interview that can help you easily rule out people that are not the right fit. Questions may include salary expectations, questions around culture fit, and a more detailed job description to query with the candidates if they are definitely interested in that role.

- Conduct interviews. Team interviews can be particularly helpful with this task. Getting input from different viewpoints on the candidate's fit for the team, can help you spot things you wouldn't have thought about on your own. Make sure everyone comes prepared to the interview ready with questions to draw out information that will lead them to answers about whether they fit on the team, in the role, and in the culture.

- Check backgrounds and references. Usually background checks and reference checks will be completed by your human resources departments. Although there is limited information that can be gleaned from these checks, you can at least validate the information the person listed on their resume is correct.

- Don't jump to hire the employee most like you or your team. Sometimes interviews end up being a popularity contest of who gets along best with the team. Try to be cognizant of that pitfall as you walk through the process. Consider these things:

    - Is the candidate competent? Does the employee have all the skills necessary to perform the role and is there another employee who may have a better skill set for the role?

    - Is the candidate capable? Is this person able to complete tasks efficiently, effectively, and on time? Will they be about to think with creativity and outside of the box? Is this person capable of growing and taking on more responsibility if needed?

    - Is the candidate compatible? Does he/she get along with the team? Will he/she get along with internal and external clients and partners? Will this person get along with you and take direction from you?

- Is this candidate committed? Is this candidate committed for the long term or are they looking for a short stop until their next destination? Does the candidate have a history of job hopping or staying in a role?

- Does the candidate have the right kind of character for our organization? Do they have values similar to yours? Are they a team player? Are they honest and trustworthy? Are they reliable?

- Does the candidate fit into your organization's culture? Considering your organization's mission, vision, and values, are they in alignment with delivering on those things? Do they express similar values to those of the organization? Will they follow organization policies and procedures?

- Is the compensation package offered satisfactory to the candidate? This is key to ensuring a high performing employee. If the compensation package is not right for them, they will feel underappreciated and will not be motivated to do their best work.

Figure 16.2

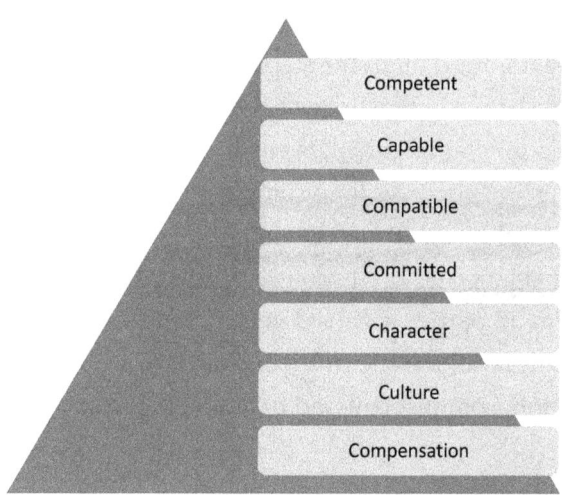

The Right Employee

Other less common activities may be part of the selection process. The use of these activities is dependent upon the type of role being filled.

- **Written tests** – Written tests may be used such as aptitude tests, personality tests, intelligence tests, etc. These tests are objective ways to judge the candidate's abilities.

- **Medical examination** – Medical examinations may be required for some positions to ensure the employee is fit to work. This can help to indicate if absenteeism could be an issue.

16.5 Onboarding New Employees

You have followed all of the steps above and have obtained the perfect candidate. Your challenge now is to retain that employee. The first step in retaining them is ensuring a thorough onboarding process. Onboarding includes orientation and placement critical to the new employee's absorption into the organization's culture as well as their specific job responsibilities and expectations. This process helps all parties involved get a better feel for whether this move is the right fit. If done right, onboarding can help increase job satisfaction, commitment and breed high performers with low attrition.

The first step in the process is to build a diagram that guides the new employee through their process. Having documentation including both wording and pictures caters to different types of learners and in some cases helps them to socialize with the company's culture faster.

Figure 16.3

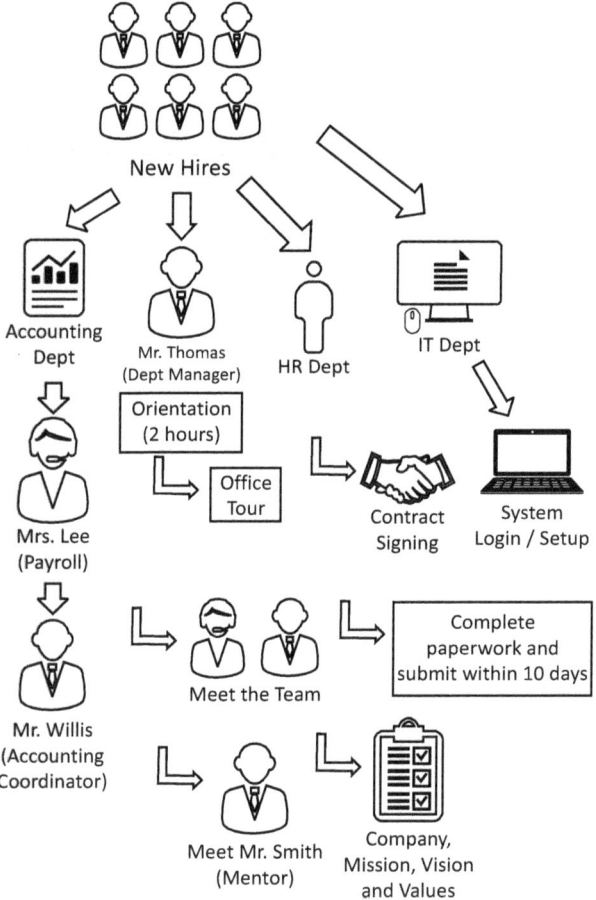

Orientation starts before the employee begins their first day of work. It starts with the first contact. If a team member reaches out to talk to the employee and welcome them to the team that is the beginning of a positive onboarding experience. Have an agenda ready for the new employee's first week at work and provide them an organizational chart so they know who-is-who. Technology can be utilized as part of onboarding too. If your team has a social media page, invite the new employee to participate. Utilize instant messenger to let the employee know you hope they have a great day. These are all things that will help a new employee assimilate better and feel included in the team.

Keep tabs on how the new employee's orientation process is going by setting up meetings at 30, 60, and 90-day intervals. Use the guidance below to plan these reviews.

- **First 30 days review** – The new team member is assimilating to his/her new environment. The employee is attending training, meeting other team members and other people in the organization, learning about the organization's offerings, and learning policies and procedures. Ask questions like:

    - Do you have access to all the resources you need?
    - What have you learned about thus far?
    - What gaps are there that we need to fill in?
    - What do you want to know more about?
    - How do you feel you are fitting in?
    - Do you have any other questions or concerns?

- **First 60 days review** – The team member is not so new anymore. He or she is getting familiar with the industry competitors, best practices, developing relationships with colleagues and teammates, getting ideas of goals to obtain, continuing training, learning about other departments, and looking at system efficiencies. At this check in, ask questions like:

    - What have you learned?

- What observations have you made?
- What have you seen that we could be better at?
- What goals do you want to set for the next check in?
- What resources do you need access to?
- Do you have someone you would like to mentor you?
- Add any feedback for matters that need to be addressed immediately.

- **First 90 days review** – At this point, the team member has really assimilated into everyday life at the organization. They are working on new projects assigned, implementing new strategies and procedures and any other work assigned. At this check in, the focus is on how the employee has been performing. There are fewer questions and more feedback dialogue. Include things in your discussion such as:
  - Obtain feedback from team members and colleagues and provide this information to the employee.
  - Include your observations of performance and assimilation to the environment.
  - Ask how they feel they have progressed to the goal they set in their last meeting and provide your feedback as well.
  - For any areas of improvement, document clear plans on actions for the employee to take to improve.

16.6 Performance Management

A key activity for every manager is managing the performance of their employees to ensure they are helping in meeting organizational goals and objectives. Performance management is the term typically used to include activities such as goal setting, continuously reviewing employee progress, feedback and coaching, developing employees, and rewarding their achievements. The main objectives of performance management are:

- Provide resources for the employee to excel at their work and become a high-level performer

- Assist in identifying knowledge gaps and work with the employee to help fill those gaps

- Encourage, empower, motivate, and reward employees

- Encourage upward and downward communication between employee and managers on a regular basis to promote understanding of performance expectations and organizational goals.

- Assist with removing barriers to effective and high-level performance

- Promote personal growth with a development plan clearly outlining skill sets and experience to take them to the next level.

Conducting performance management on a regular basis has several benefits. First, the organization typically sees better performance because employees really understand their role and appreciate knowing where they stand. Employee retention and loyalty is improved as well as productivity. Common barriers of communication are removed. Responsibility and accountability is clear for all parties involved.

For the manager, performance management saves time and reduces conflicts. As the manager and employee meet on a frequent basis, communication becomes easier. It ensures performance efficiency and consistency because employees are getting feedback on a virtually real time basis.

The employee benefits from performance management because clear expectations of their performance are set and communicated. Career paths become less of a secret and more of a clear outlined path to follow to success. This promotes job satisfaction.

Conducting a Performance Management Plan

If not designed well, a performance management plan can result in reduced employee satisfaction, productivity, and ultimately attrition. There are clear steps each manager will want to go through to establish an effective performance management plan for each employee.

Figure 16.4

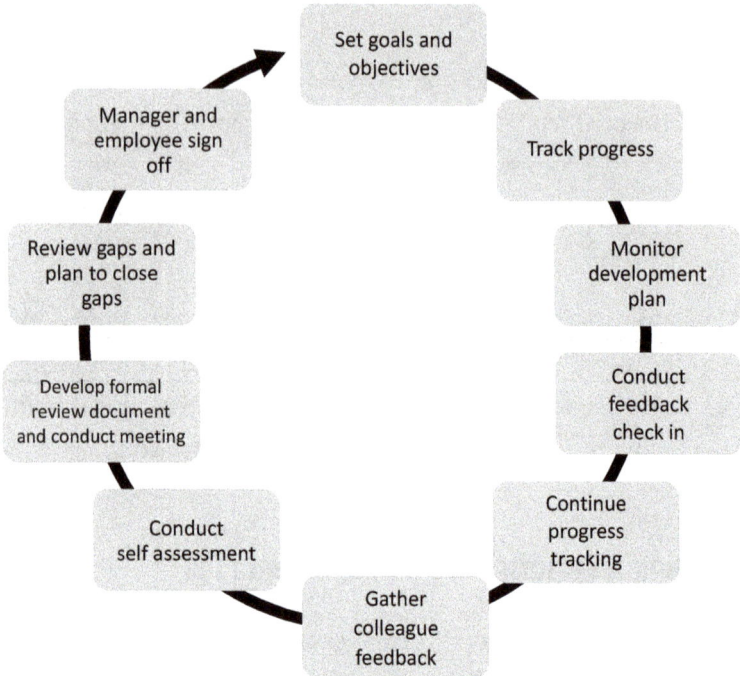

- The first step is to set clear goals and objectives for the employee to achieve. Work with the employee to develop any action plans to help achieve those goals.

- Track employee progress to completion of actions to meet goals and objectives.

- Review the employee's current development plan to determine if any additional training or experience is needed to reach their goals.

- Check with the employee providing feedback on what they are doing well, what you want them to continue doing, what you want them to start doing, and what you want them to stop doing. This method is a simple way to outline exactly what needs to be done to get them to succeed in their formal review.

- Continue tracking employee progress to completion of actions that were updated in the previous step.

- Gather feedback from teammates and other colleagues in the organization. This feedback gives you perspectives you may not have considered. Review the validity and appropriateness of the feedback and organize it for the formal review.

- Ask the employee to complete a self-assessment. How do they feel they have performed to their goals thus far? What are their strengths? What are their weaknesses?

- Pull together feedback previously gathered, self-assessment, and your own observations into a formal document for the employee's performance review. Conduct the meeting sharing their accomplishments and feedback for improvements.

- Identify where there are gaps in performance and work with the employee to create an action plan to close those gaps.

- Both the manager and the employee sign off on the plan to demonstrate agreement and understanding of next steps.

Chapter Summary

- People management is obtaining, utilizing, and retaining a team of people who are satisfied with their jobs.

- A human resource manager is responsible for planning, staffing, recruiting new talent, selecting appropriate candidates, and developing/training new employees.

- Common sources of external recruiting are employment at the organizational level, advertisements, employment exchanges, employment agencies, educational institutions, recommendations and labor contractors.

- To select the right employees, recruiters develop a clear job description, develop a recruitment strategy, organize a hiring checklist, consider internal applications, carefully review applications and credentials, complete pre-screening interviews, conduct interviews, perform background and reference checks, and refrain from hiring someone who reminds you of yourself.

- To aid in ensuring employee retention, organizations must develop a beneficial on-boarding process.

- A performance management plan consists of setting goals and objectives, tracking the progress, monitoring the development plan, conducting feedback check ins, gather colleague feedback, conduct a self-assessment, develop formal documentation, conduct the review, review and plan to close gaps, and obtain the required sign offs (manager and employee).

Quiz

1. When you estimate the <u>optimal level of staffing required</u> for a project, task, or goal, you need to consider :
   i. How many people are needed,
   ii. What skill sets are needed
   iii. When are they needed
   iv. How long they are needed
   v. Why are they needed - which of the following option is correct?

   a. Options (i) to (iv) are valid
   b. All options are valid
   c. Options (i) to (iii) are valid
   d. Options (ii) to (v) are valid

2. Which of the pair of activities on the staffing process and one of their salient features <u>is wrong</u>?

   a. Selection – Screen candidates according to skill set
   b. Orientation – Placing the right person in the right position
   c. Training and development – Training is only needed at the time of joining and not periodically
   d. Remuneration – Often related to work performance, skill set, etc.

3. Which of the following statements is true about staffing challenges?

   a) HR Planning is one of the costliest processes in an organization

   b. Manpower need not be utilized to its optimal capacity

   c. Moving an unqualified person from a higher position to a lower position is easier than moving a highly skilled worker to a higher position.

   d. Depression is not at all a cause for absenteeism in the industry today.

4. Which of the following descriptions is correct pertaining to common sources of external recruitment?

   a. Labor contractor: A dedicated contractor engaged by an organization to recruit suitable candidates

   b. Recommendations: Recruitment based on recommendation letters from influential persons of the society

   c) Employment agencies: They recruit people to facilitate organizations that meet their manpower needs.

   d. Employment exchanges: Swapping of employment from one company to another.

5. Which of the following pairs **is wrong** about selecting the right employee?

   a. Considering internal applicants and building a talent pool

   b. Reviewing applications and credentials and weeding out those not meeting minimum eligibility requirements

   c. ⟳ Conducting pre-screening interviews and picking up inappropriate candidates and training them

   d. Checking backgrounds and references and validation of information in the resume

| **Answers** | 1 – a | 2 – c | 3 – a | 4 – c | 5 – c |

This page is intentionally left blank

Chapter 17

Customer Relationship Management

Up to now there has been a lot of detail on managing our internal customers. Our internal customers are top level managers, teams, colleagues, and employees. As we begin to conclude our review of management essentials topics, we will focus on managing our external customers. External customers are our consumers, clients and partners.

Relationships with external customers are typically managed with customer relationship management. This is a strategy to solidify our relationships with our clients. This system reduces cost, time, enhances productivity and profitability in an organization. The system collects all the data from all over the organization regarding our clients and places them in a central location that employees can access when needed. This system not only collects data on our existing clients, but also captures our relationships with prospective clients.

> Key learning objectives of this chapter include the reader's understanding of the following:
> - Stages of customer relationships
> - Types of customers
> - Customer orientation
> - Steps to ensure quality customer relationships
> - Measurement of customer relationships

An effective customer relationship management system has the following features:

- Identifies client needs including likes and dislikes

- Documents client response activities to any inquiries or requests. This includes both positive and negative interactions with the client.

- Measures the client's level of satisfaction by feedback from the client.

- Measures the client's level of loyalty by looking at whether the client would recommend our organization, how often they come for return business, are they going to competitors for any needs, etc.

- Promotes customer retention.

- Tracks customer complaints and how they were handled.

- Delivers information and services through customer service.

Customer relationship management systems are important because they provide a wealth of knowledge on clients in one spot that can easily be analyzed and acted upon. It reduces redundancies between departments since each department is not managing its own customer files. The system provides a mechanism to review the progress you have made with a customer. You can look at their full history with the company. Customer relationship systems are also very cost effective and helpful in tracking new relationships with potential customers.

Figure 17.1

17.1 Defining Customer Relationship

Dictionary.com defines relationship as the way in which two or more people are connected. Relationships evolve over time. Think about the relationships in your life. Your best friend was not your best friend the first day you met. The relationship evolved over time. The same concept applies for customer relationships. Below is an outline of the evolution relationships typically go through.

Figure 17.2

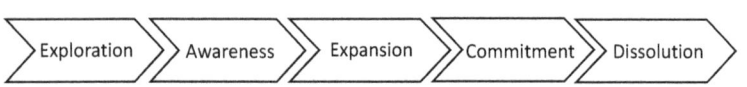

- **Exploration** – The prospective client is investigating or testing your organization's capabilities and performance. They are comparing to industry standards and performance to competitors. At the same time, they are looking at the product's or brand's usefulness and asking, "Is this really worth it?"

- **Awareness** – The prospective client has an understanding of the motivational values of the organization or their products.

- **Expansion** – The customer puts their faith in your organization and agrees to do business with you. A relationship of interdependence is formed. At this time, expansion of services and products is a great possibility.

- **Commitment** – Your organization now understands what business rules your client operates under. You work to follow those roles and to not just meet their needs but go above and beyond.

- **Dissolution** – The relationship ends with the client. The customer no longer needs the services your organization offers and begins to look for better perspectives.

17.2 Types of Customers

Since customers are such a critical part of an organization's business, it is important to understand customers can be categorized into groups to better demonstrate their value. In order to properly manage your customers, identifying which group your customer belongs in essential. The categories of groups the customer can fall into are as follows:

Figure 17.3

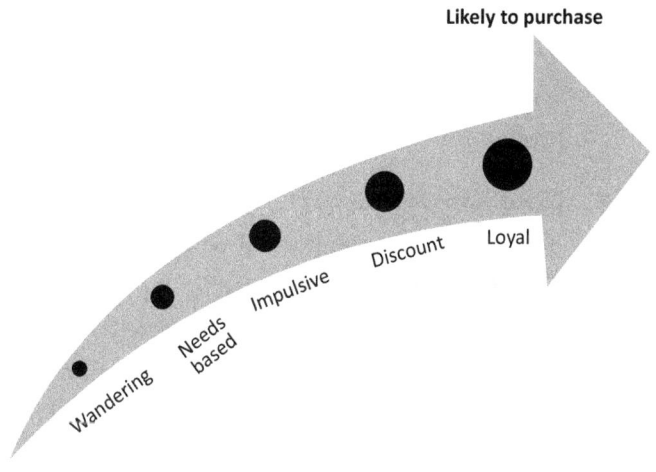

- **Loyal customers** – Loyal customers will act as advocates for your organization. They refer customers to you and they act as references to contact for prospective customers. These customers repeatedly contact your organization for business, so it is imperative you stay in touch with them regularly. They expect prompt response and attention and recognition of their loyalty to you.

- **Discount customers** – Discount customers may visit you frequently but only when you are offering a discount on services. In fact, the better the discount, the more likely they are to purchase from you. Beware of these customers because there is a risk they will quickly jump to a competitor if a better discount is offered.

- **Impulsive customers** – These customers are driven by the urge to buy. They don't necessarily have a particular need they need to meet or a product to buy but they have the urge to buy. These customers can prove challenging because they don't know what they want, so it is difficult to pinpoint what they may purchase. The good thing about these customers is if you are able to find something that piques their interest, there is a high probability that they will purchase a lot.

- **Need based customers** – These customers have a specific need they are seeking to fill with your organization. They tend to purchase a specific product and nothing more. It is difficult to transition these customers over to purchasing other products in your product line. These types of customers are not necessarily loyal to your organization so if they experience a negative interaction, they may look for other prospects.

- **Wandering customers** – These customers are window shoppers and are the least profitable. They are not really sure what they want to buy and are really just gathering information on products for comparison and needs analysis.

17.3 Customer Orientation

Another aspect of customers you should be aware of is their orientation. What are they most concerned about? Knowing this will allow you to better sell to the customer as well as meet their customer service needs.

- **Cost oriented** – These customers are most concerned about cost even if they have to sacrifice efficacy, performance or quality. They typically end up buying the lowest cost product which sometimes leaves them with a loss. They are also quick to blame the supplier when a product they purchased failed rather than looking at the low cost they paid resulting in lower quality. These customers also are known to purchase secondhand products and expect them to work as new as well as use local vendors to fix products at lower cost and lesser quality. Both of these expectations result in a failure of the product and the customer turns to the supplier to fix the issue. Therefore, these customers can be very costly.

- **Value oriented** – These customers are looking for the most efficient and high performing products. They are willing to invest higher dollars for the value they receive from a longer running product. In fact, these customers recognize making a premium investment could result in cost savings in the future, so they are willing to spend the money. Since these customers will spend money for quality products, they tend to be satisfied customers with good relationships with their suppliers.

- **Technology oriented** – These customers look for the best technology regardless of cost, quality, or performance. Their outlook is technology is changing so often it is in their best interest staying with the latest technology will help them sustain productivity. This is the ideal customer for suppliers frequently releasing the latest and greatest technologies. They are innovative and interested in trying the newest thing out. These customers are typically satisfied customers and have good relationships with their suppliers due to frequent referrals.

17.4 Ensuring Quality Customer Relationships

Your organization needs customers to sustain everyday business and grow. Therefore, it is vitally important you take time to examine your customer relationships and ensure they are beneficial for both parties. Most important to a good customer relationship is providing quality goods and services efficiently and effectively. If you can demonstrate to your customer you can do this better than your competitors, you can win a trustworthy and loyal relationship with a customer. Trust in the relationship gives confidence and security to both parties. Commitment indicates a mutual long-term relationship where both parties work together to uphold the relationship.

Other characteristics of a high-quality relationship are:

- **Courtesy** – Even when a customer becomes annoyed and even rude due to different reasons, it is imperative that the supplier keeps their cool. Remaining calm and sympathizing with the issue will help in driving customer satisfaction.

- **Availability** – Some customers prefer to speak to a person rather than through email, voicemail, or electronic responses. Therefore, it is ideal to have a human contact they can easily get in touch with should they have questions or concerns. This also helps develop a relationship with the customer that is an emotional bond that helps to drive more business.

- **Responsive** – Prompt response and follow-up to questions and concerns goes a long way in a customer relationship. Lack of response and follow-up can also break a customer relationship and cause customers to go to another vendor.

- **Intelligent** – Customers are looking for a good deal including discounts and reasonable prices. Suppliers should be strategic in their ability to offer discounted prices to customers to avoid the customer going to a competitor for a better price.

- **Futuristic** – Try to stay up to date with technological changes. As technology evolves, some services and products will become obsolete. Also, if you aren't careful, competitors will develop solutions and services more compatible with newer technologies resulting in customers going to the competitor.

17.4 Measuring Customer Relationships

How do you quantify your relationships with your customers rather than it being a subjective feeling? Understanding the strength of the relationships you have with your customers helps you plan your next steps to take. Strengthening relationships means that you want to do activities that will add to long term success rather than just short-term wins with the customer. Essentially you are investing in customer success instead of customer support.

Customer success takes into account the long-term relationship. It works proactively anticipate issues and needs before the customer voices them. The goal is to help the customer get as much value from the product or service as they can. We want to help the customer generate revenue with our product.

Customer support focuses on the short term. It is reacting to customer concerns or issues as they come up. The main goal is to address the issue occurring with the product. This does not help the customer generate revenue.

Figure 17.4

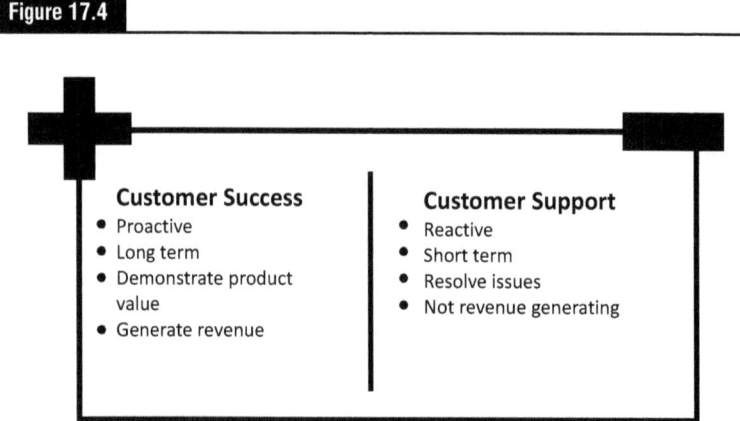

As we look at measuring customer relationships, we want to put our primary focus on measuring customer success. There are several customer success metrics being measured in various industries today. Let's take a look at some of the more popular ones.

Churn

Your customer churn rate is defined as the percentage of customers who decide to discontinue use of your product during a specific period of time. There are actually three different types of churn rate organizations typically calculate on a monthly basis. The first is the customer churn rate previously described.

Next, is the gross dollar churn rate which is the percentage of your total revenues that are lost because your customer downgrades to a less expensive option. Third, is the monthly recurring revenue churn (aka net MRR churn) which is the net dollar churn, but it also takes into account the gains that come from customers who purchase additional or upgrade their products.

Figure 17.5

Customer churn %
- number of customers lost in a specified month/number of customers you had at the end of the previous month

Net dollar churn or MRR churn %
- revenue lost from customer churn and downselling in a specified month/revenue from the end of the previous month

Net MRR churn%
- revenue lost from customer churn and downselling -upselling or cross-selling in a specified month/revenue from the end of the previous month

Once you have collected these numbers, what does it all mean? Let's take a look at a graph comparing the three types of churn in a sample business.

Figure 17.6

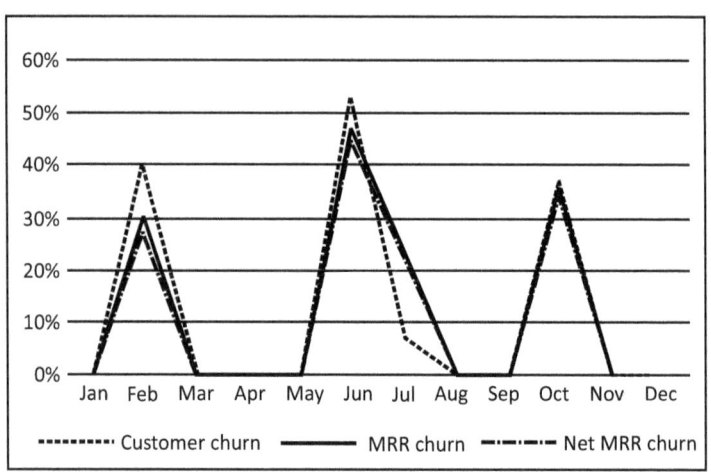

When you look at this chart, you cannot see the entire picture just by looking at customer churn. Looking at July, you see the customer churn rate was only 7%. That sounds good, right? Looking at the MRR churn we see it is a rather large 25% indicating a customer left us who was paying us high dollars. Essentially, this shows us how the dissolution of one high paying customer can really affect our business.

Organizations usually set a goal for a customer churn rate below 5%, and MRR churn rate below 1% if they choose to be best-in-class.

You can gather more information by looking at the actual dollars as well. When you look at dollars, you are putting an actual amount to your churn rates which can indicate to you just how bad your issue is. For example, if you have a small customer base, the loss of one customer can fluctuate the numbers significantly when you look at percentages. When you look at the actual dollars, you see a better picture that can help you determine if this is really an issue you need to work on.

Expansion Revenue

Expansion revenue is another helpful measurement to look at when judging the success of your customer relationships. It gives you an idea of the percentage of new revenue coming from your existing customers. Where churn measures for retention, expansion measures how well you are able to get your client to grow with your products and solutions. Measuring expansion revenue on a monthly basis is called expansion MRR. Calculate expansion MRR as follows:

Figure 17.7

Expansion MRR
- new revenue from upselling and cross-selling in a specified month/revenue you had at the end of the previous month

What does expansion MRR tell you about the bigger picture of your organization? Take a look at the graph below.

Figure 17.8

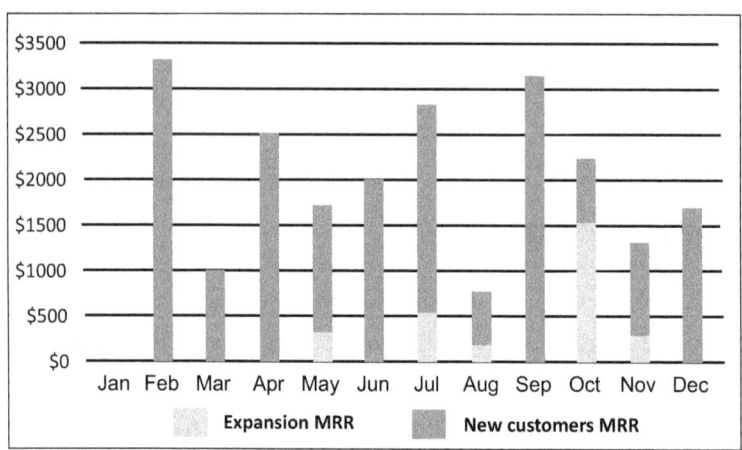

The dark bars are sales achieved by the sales team. The light bars indicate how well you are doing with your customer or your customer success. In the ideal scenario, the expansion MRR is so large a negative net MRR churn rate is achieved. When this is accomplished, you can grow your revenue even if you cannot get new customers.

The typical goal for expansion MRR in most industries is to offset the churn rate with the expansion MRR and make the MRR churn negative.

Customer Satisfaction

We have looked at metrics that tell us what the customer's actions have been. We know if they have been leaving us or if they have been buying more from us. The gap we have is understanding how the customer is feeling towards our products and company. If you can identify customers whose feelings are not satisfactory, your organization can develop plans to address their concerns and put the relationship in good standing.

Net Promoter Score

Net promoter score is widely used to measure customer satisfaction today. It is a very simple tool to use in that you ask the customer one question – "How likely are you to recommend our product/service/organization to your friends?" The customer chooses a number between 0 and 10. 0 indicates "unlikely to recommend at all" and 10 indicates "will definitely recommend." The responses are gathered and categorized into three groups:

- 0 – 6 = Detractors, people who will not recommend your product and may even give your product bad reviews to others
- 7 – 8 = Passives, people who think the product is acceptable but probably will not be an active advocate of how great your products are.
- 9 – 10 = Promoters, people who are very happy with your products and will refer your products to their friends and family
- Net Promoter Score (NPS) is calculated as follows:

Figure 17.9

Net Promoter Score
- % promoters - % detractors

NPS is a great indicator for your potential for growth. It also forecasts your customer loyalty. Your goal is to move your passive scorers to promoters. Detractors are typically more difficult to move so most companies focus on their passive scorers to improve their customer loyalty and therefore potential for growth.

NPS goals vary by organization and industry. 50 is typically viewed as good but it is recommended to look at NPS scores of your competitors for comparison. For example, if my organization manufactures mp3 players, I may strive for an NPS score of 90 since Apple's latest score was 89.

Customer Satisfaction Score (CSAT)

When you look at the customer satisfaction score, you focus more on their short term happiness with your product or solution. At the time of taking the survey, how satisfied was the customer with your solution?

In a CSAT survey, there is usually a question that asks, "What is your overall satisfaction with (product/service/organization)?" The customer is asked to rate from 1 to 5 where 1 is very unsatisfied, 2 is unsatisfied, 3 is neutral, 4 is satisfied, and 5 is very satisfied. The surveys are collected and feedback from this question calculated into a percentage. The end result is a percentage of customers that answered either satisfied or very satisfied.

Figure 17.10

Customer Satifaction Score (CSAT)
- % of customers who responded satified and 5 very sasafied

If you received a score of 75%, it would mean that 75 out of the 100 customers who took the survey were satisfied or very satisfied.

A common goal for CSAT in most industries is 80%.

Chapter Summary

- Customer relationship management focuses on customer loyalty, retention, satisfaction, response, complaints, service, and needs.

- The three types of customer orientations are cost (pricing over all traits), value (most efficient and high performing), and technology.

- The five characteristics for quality customer relationships are courtesy, availability, responsiveness, intelligence, and futuristic.

- Customer relationships are measured through success and support.

- Customer churn rate is the percent of customers who decide to discontinue use of your product.

- To effectively understand the churn rate, companies should also compare Monthly Recurring Revenue (MRR) and Net MRR churn.

- Expansion revenue depicts the percentage of new revenue coming from existing customers.

Quiz

1. These customers may prove challenging because they don't know what they want, so it is difficult to pinpoint what they may purchase.

    a. Impulsive customers

    b. Need-based customers

    c. Wandering customers

    d. Discount customers

2. Which of the following sentences is wrong?

    a. Customers who are only concerned about cost, irrespective of efficacy, performance, or quality are called 'cost oriented.'

    b. Customers who look for efficiency and high performance in the products they purchase are called 'value-oriented.'

    c. Customers who look for the best technology regardless of cost, quality, or performance are called 'technology oriented.'

    d. Customer orientation knowledge is useful for the exploitation of weaknesses of customers and to make quick money.

3. 'When the customer is annoyed, remaining calm and sympathizing with the issue will help drive customer satisfaction'- is a description of which of the following characteristics?

   a. Responsive

   b. Intelligent

   c. Courtesy

   d. Futuristic

4. Which of the following statements is wrong?

   a. Understanding the strength of customer relationships helps to plan the next steps

   b. It is possible to quantify relationships with customers though it is a subjective feeling

   c. Customer success takes into account only the short-term relationship

   d. Customer support focuses on reacting to customer concerns or issues as they emerge

5. Which of the following options is correct?
   i. CSAT helps in measuring only short-term happiness about the product or service
   ii. Net promoter score talks about 'How likely are you to recommend our product/service/organization to your friends'
   iii. Customer satisfaction talks about understanding how the customer is feeling towards our products and company.
   iv. Customer churn rate is defined as the percentage of customers who decide to discontinue the use of your product during a specific period of time.

   a. (i) only

   b. (ii), (iii) (iv) only

   c. (i) and (ii) only

   d. (i) and (iii) only

| Answers | 1 – a | 2 – d | 3 – c | 4 – c | 5 – b |

This page is intentionally left blank

Chapter 18

International Business and Management

The prior chapters have prepared you to manage and lead a profitable company where employees look forward to going to work on Monday mornings. Your skill in inspiring your staff to go beyond what they think they are capable of, and your thorough planning, organizing, leading, and controlling, are key to your management's success and will also be useful when you lead an International business.

Key learning objectives of this chapter include the reader's understanding of the following:

- Need of international trade?
- Forms of global business
- Difference between domestic and international business
- Traits of an international manager

Today, it is unwise to restrict a business within one's own geographical borders since approximately 95% of the world's population is outside the United States. You wouldn't want to write a business plan that excludes 95% of your potential customers, would you? Therefore, it is important to have skills to manage a business internationally. Business leaders with international expertise are always in high demand. According to Management Recruiters, international experience is also sought after because it shows employers that the manager has learned independence, resourcefulness, and entrepreneurship.

The tools and skills that are necessary for international business managers include risk analysis, market research, expansion strategy, critical thinking, humility, cultural awareness, communication, and an awareness of expressions that are often not understood in our own culture such as "saving face" in China or "sobremesa" in Spain.

18.1 Why is International Trade Needed?

Why is England not known for great wine or Portugal for superior wool? There is a reason why countries specialize in what they do well, based on education, labor costs, climate, and access to resources. A nation that is more efficient than anyone else in the production of any good or service is said to have an absolute advantage in the production of that good or service. Adam Smith in 1776 called this "Absolute Advantage" and argued that trying to be self-sufficient and produce all goods in one's own country was inefficient and led to a lower standard of living. His argument is more obvious now than ever before.

Portugal has an absolute advantage over England in producing grapes and wine because Portugal has better soil, water, weather, and lower labor costs. England has an absolute advantage over Portugal in raising sheep and producing wool due to its climate, landscape, and infrastructure. It costs England more to grow grapes in an acre of land that could instead be used to raise high-quality sheep. By specializing, England produces more wool than it can use and Portugal produces more wine than it can drink. When both countries trade, England gets more (and better) wine and Portugal gets more (and better) wool than either country could produce on its own. International trade enhances lives by making the products that we buy of higher quality and providing them at a lower cost.

18.2 Forms of Global Business

Companies have a choice in the way that they reach customers outside their borders.

- Exporting
- Licensing
- Franchising
- Joint Venture
- Wholly owned affiliate

Exporting – Exporting is when you ship your product from your own country to other countries. It is a low-cost and lower-risk approach, making you less dependent on domestic sales. The disadvantages are the cost of duties/tariffs, shipping costs, and the lead time to get your product to the market.

Licensing – Licensing allows a domestic company (the licensor) to receive royalty payments for allowing another company (the licensee) to produce its products, sell its services, or use its brand name in a particular foreign market. Advantages of this method include market expansion without investing more money, avoiding trade barriers such as duties/tariffs, and no shipping. The disadvantages, however, are that you are giving up control over marketing and product quality and are teaching your licensee all they need to learn to become your competitor when your agreement ends.

Franchising – A company that makes or markets a product or a service (the licensor) can franchise or license that business enterprise to another organization (the licensee). In most cases, the licensee must follow strict guidelines so that their product is identical to that of the licensor. McDonald's and KFC are the best examples of franchises. Both the companies have opened franchises across the world. Advantages of this method include a faster way to enter foreign markets and giving a franchisor additional cash flow without a large investment. Disadvantages include some loss of control and the possible risk of harm to the brand if a foreign franchisee devalues the product.

Joint Venture – When companies combine key resources, costs, risks, technology, and people to complete a specific task, it is called a joint venture. Advantages of joint ventures include the avoidance of trade barriers such as duties and tariffs, each company bearing only part of the costs. The disadvantages are that the profits have to be shared and it becomes difficult to merge the cultures of two companies (particularly in different countries).

Wholly owned affiliate – Foreign offices, facilities, and manufacturing plants are 100 percent owned by the parent company. Advantages are that the parent company receives all of the profits and has complete control. Disadvantages are that it is expensive and loss is borne by the parent company.

18.3 Domestic vs. International Business: What is the Difference?

- Currencies
- Local taste/preferences
- Political risk
- Cultural barriers
- Language

Currencies – At home, your business is primarily concerned with one currency, but exchange rates will affect your international business' success. When the U.S. dollar appreciates against the Euro, American goods become more expensive to Europeans, thereby decreasing your European sales.

Local taste/Preferences – Do you opt for consistency or adaptation? Should you export your product exactly as is without changing anything, or adapt it to local preferences? That depends on the product itself. If you are Tesla or Warner music, your products can be identical in other countries (if you are Tesla you'll have to change the steering wheel in England, however). If you are McDonald's, beef burgers won't be welcome in India where Hindus worship the cows as sacred.

Political risk – A country's corruption and instability may make it a high-risk country for foreign companies. On the other hand, a country with low corruption and friendly to business makes it a safer and more attractive market.

Cultural barriers – Because an understanding of a country's culture is complex and key to a successful international business, the topic will be treated later in this chapter in greater detail.

Language – In a world where Google Translate has become ubiquitous, monolingual speakers may underestimate the power of a foreign language. It will open new doors of opportunities by eliciting the admiration and respect of the citizens of that country. But mistakes in advertisements, instruction manuals, and product descriptions can result in poor sales, offending potential customers or simply giving your company a reputation for lack of detail. A recent example is of a mosquito repellent device on sale that read the following copy on its advertising and packaging: "Electron go out mosquito small a night lamp" or the Swedish vacuum cleaner company Electrolux who mistakenly marketed to American consumers with the tagline: "Nothing sucks like an Electrolux."

18.4 Cultural Differences

We acquire national culture primarily by growing up in a certain country. Depending on where you grew up, what exposure you had to people and friends from other cultures, and how much you may have traveled, your values and identification are often shared with others from your country. Dutch sociologist and Professor of Anthropology and International Management, Geert Hofstede, was the pioneer of research that led to an understanding of cultural differences between countries. We must consider that the world has changed in substantial ways since Hofstede's research and conclusions, but his findings still offer a helpful guide. He found consistent cultural dimensions across countries: power distance, individualism/collectivism, masculinity/femininity, uncertainty avoidance, short-term/long-term orientation, and indulgence/restraint. Hofstede described power distance as how much acceptance people in a country show for the distribution of power in their society or organizations. Scandinavian countries exhibit low power distance: employees don't like their boss to have excessive power over them. They want more autonomy and power while the opposite is true in countries such as Russia and India.

Individualism refers to self-sufficiency and the importance society gives to the individual. In individualistic societies, employees place loyalty to the company or the group second, and to themselves first. The U.S is high in individualism while China is low. In China, employees cooperate and exhibit a collective emphasis on achieving goals.

Masculinity/femininity refers to how roles are distributed between genders, but also to the difference between societies that are more assertive and competitive (masculine) and those that are more nurturing and cooperative (feminine). Japan and the U.S. are masculine, while The Netherlands and Sweden are feminine.

Uncertainty avoidance refers to the degree to which a society is willing to ensure a predictable environment, versus a more ambiguous or unreliable one. Countries with strong uncertainty avoidance, like Greece and Portugal, seek security rather than uncertainty.

Short-term/long-term orientation separates countries into those that prefer immediate gratification, and those that are comfortable with sacrificing in the present for a better future. Countries with short-term orientations are more consumer-driven, whereas countries with long-term orientations plan more for the future and are likely to save more and spend less.

Indulgence/restraint considers how much we value and act upon our impulses and whether our spendings reflect our indulgence by purchase of items unnecessary to our basic needs. The U.S., Canada, and Australia are higher in indulgence than The Netherlands, Italy, and France.

High-Context vs. Low-Context cultures: In a high-context culture, the listeners are intuitive, non-verbal expression is given more importance, and people rely heavily on situational cues for meaning when communicating with others. Relationships are important in high-context cultures, your word is more valued than written agreements, and rushing to close a deal isn't welcome. Some examples include Japan, China, and Mexico. In a low-context culture, the speaker must clarify his intent, and emphasis is given to written and spoken words. Written agreements are binding and directness and confrontation are expected. Some examples include the U.S., Germany, and the United Kingdom.

To navigate the rapids of cultures, you need to inculcate cultural awareness, focus on becoming more flexible, listen more, and speak less. Learning the language of that country helps not only with communication but will help you gain the respect of the citizens of that country.

18.5 What type of an International Manager should you be?

Your goal is to become a geocentric manager and to avoid becoming an ethnocentric or a polycentric manager.

An ethnocentric manager is the "we know best" type, managing under the belief that their native country, its culture, work ethic, and behavior are all superior to that of other countries. Often, (but not always) this approach and beliefs are a result of their lack of exposure. It is an absurd belief to think that one's own country is the best in everything for no other reason than that we were born in it.

Polycentric Managers swing in the opposite direction of ethnocentrics, their motto being "they know best." They believe that managers in foreign offices best understand their native culture and practices and should be left alone by the home office. While part of their thinking is sound that natives know their culture best, there is a history and breadth of experience at the headquarters that can be used to avoid mistakes, increase profits and maximize results in other countries.

Geocentric Managers take the wise and balanced approach that "what is best is what's effective, regardless of its origin." They are the most successful international managers because they take a cafeteria approach of using the talent, resources, and advantages of each country that works best to achieve organizational goals.

18.6 How to Choose Where to Expand Internationally

Easy access to growing markets is the most important factor used by a multinational company for determining if a country or a region has an attractive business climate. Depending on your chosen form of international sales, there are qualitative factors to consider such as workforce quality, infrastructure such as ports, airports, highways, and warehousing, as well as your company's strategy. Quantitative factors to consider are the kind of facilities being built/leased, trade barriers that include duties and tariffs (but could also take the form of import quotas), and transportation and labor costs. If you need bilingual or multilingual staff (for example, in your customer service) then The Netherlands with its multilingual population would be a better choice than England where fewer people speak a second or third language.

Chapter Summary

- 95% of the world's population lives outside of the United States and as a result, customers beyond your borders can be the biggest share of your sales.

- International Management careers are among the highest paid and most fulfilling with companies valuing those with International experience as leaders who possess skills like independence, resourcefulness, and entrepreneurship.

- Specialization by countries encourages trade and results in a higher standard of living by lowering costs, increasing competition and quality, and expanding choice.

- Forms of Global Business include exporting, licensing, franchising, joint venture, and wholly-owned affiliate. Each has its own advantages and disadvantages to consider.

- International managers recognize the additional layers required for an international business vs. a domestic business, including currencies, adaptation, political risk, cultural barriers, and language.

- An understanding of cultural differences is key to international success. Professor Gert Hofstede's study of cultural dimensions helps us identify what is necessary to understand each type of culture.

- Is your next business meeting with a person from a high-context or low-context culture? Identifying which and conducting business accordingly, can make or break the deal.

- Geocentric managers get better results by taking advantage of what is superior in each market and ignoring tribalism and ethnocentric tendencies.

- Any form of global business should be coupled with choosing the most appropriate markets for your business. Easy access to growing markets is the first criteria for choosing between countries.

Quiz

1. International experience makes employers think that:

    a. the manager has learned independence, resourcefulness, and entrepreneurship

    b. the manager has learned about risk analysis and market research.

    c. the manager has humility and cultural awareness

    d. the manager has good communication and has learned about expressions

2. The disadvantages of _____ are the cost of duties/tariffs, shipping costs, and the lead time to get your product into the market.

    a. exporting

    b. licensing

    c. franchising

    d. joint venture

3. The advantage of _____ is that the parent company receives all of the profits and has complete control

    a. exporting

    b. licensing

    c. franchising

    d. wholly owned affiliate

4. Which of the following statements is wrong?

   a. When the US dollar appreciates against the Euro, American goods become cheaper to Europeans thereby increasing European sales

   b. Corruption and instability may make it a high-risk country for foreign companies

   c. Understanding the culture of a country, though a complex factor, is the key to successful international business.

   d. When the US dollar appreciates against the Euro, American goods become more expensive to Europeans thereby decreasing European sales

5. Which of the following options is correct?
   i. Polycentric Manager - They know the best
   ii. Geocentric Manager - What's best is what's effective, regardless of its origin
   iii. Ethnocentric Manager - We know the best

   a. Only (i) is correct

   b. Only (i) & (ii) are correct

   c. All three are wrong

   d. All three are correct

| Answers | 1 – a | 2 – a | 3 – d | 4 – a | 5 – d |

CPSIA information can be obtained
at www.ICGtesting.com
Printed in the USA
LVHW051140190723
752740LV00007B/221